THE HOLISTIC PRACTITIONER'S
BUSINESS BIBLE

THE
HOLISTIC
PRACTITIONER'S
BUSINESS BIBLE

Essentials for
Growing a Thriving Practice

POLLY STRONG BAUMER

SEABOARD PRESS

JAMES A. ROCK & COMPANY, PUBLISHERS

This book is dedicated

to the memory of my

beloved father

Hugh Sheldon Strong

whose spirit is with me every day

Strong by name, strong by nature

Acknowledgments

I would like to thank the following people for their contributions of knowledge and time to this project. I am especially grateful to Jeff and Diana Krauth for having the vision to create *Many Hands Magazine,* and for providing the Pioneer Valley of western Massachusetts with excellent literature for over 20 years through their bookstore, Beyond Words Bookshop; Jody Larson, editor, for all her help and her wonderful sense of humor; Patty Gates, licensed massage therapist, whose massages have brought me back to life many times; AnDréya Wilde, psychotherapist, for her wise counsel and friendship over the years; Kate Faulkner, physical therapist and human body problem solver extraordinaire; Richard Kowalski, chiropractor; Charles Brummer, M.D.; Dale Moss, homeopath; Andrew Weiss, Dean of Students at the New England School of Whole Health Education; Margi Kolchin and Linda Robinson-Hidas, acupuncturists; Mary Ellen Waletkus, accountant; Ed Etheredge, attorney; Linda Sivertsen, magazine editor; and the whole *Many Hands* community for years of inspiration and support, with special nods to Shel Berkowitz, Richard Clark, Barry and Vicki Elson, Fran Freeman, Jewell Greco, Ross Hackerson, Nannette Hucknall, Pat Joyce, Avadhan and Dick Larson, Jim Lemkin, Deborah Levy, Joann Lutz, Erin McGill, Marcy Nickerson, Kippy Phelps, Deliah Rosel, Donna Robbins, Molly Scott, Pam Smith-Selavka, Richard Shaw, Wendi Weinberg, Marcia Wolff, and Joanne Zander-Fox.

I also thank Nelson Bernard at Eagle Printing for his years of efficient service, friendship, and volunteer efforts; the wonderful folks at Whalen's Stationers and Yes Computers; and Peter DeRose, Paris Finley, and Jenny Pelissier at the Daily Hampshire Gazette.

My deep gratitude goes out to my friends who have contributed advice, encouragement, and technical information to the book: Rita Bleiman, Ann Leone, Sally Rubenstone, Pam McCarthy, Cindy Chandler-Guy, and Margi Williams, as well as to Lilda, Lynne, and Jim Rock for their extraordinary care and handling of both author and manuscript.

Finally I thank my family for supporting my efforts, especially my husband, Don, for encouraging me to take the time off to write; my son, Ben, for his computer expertise; my daughter, Maggie, for her comprehensive editing skills; and my mother, brother, and sister for the creative environment they have always fostered.

Table of Contents

Introduction

Have you ever known someone with an intractable medical condition? If so, you know the pain of watching that person struggle through the labyrinth of doctors' offices, hospitals, and pharmacies in search of a cure. Weeks, months, and years can go by without an accurate diagnosis, and the suffering continues with no relief in sight. It can be one of the most frustrating and enervating dilemmas faced by parents, siblings, children—by virtually anyone close to the patient.

From 1989 to 2005, I had the pleasure of being on the other side of these health quandaries. In my position as owner and editor of a holistic health magazine, I was frequently called by people who wanted to thank me for publishing the names of the alternative practitioners who were ultimately able to solve many of these medical mysteries. When every other traditional method of treating illness had failed, the homeopaths, chiropractors, Rolfers, massage therapists, and nutritionists were able to effect a cure. It was not uncommon for me to hear comments like, "I never would have found this person if it hadn't been for your magazine," and "We had tried everything for a whole year. If only we had gone to the acupuncturist earlier," and so on.

Prior to 1989, I gave up my position as a manager of development publications for a small New England college because my husband, a professor of political science, had won a Congressional Fellowship, and we needed to move to Alexandria, VA, for one year. I planned to spend the time thinking about what I really wanted to do job-wise when we returned to Massachusetts. Up to that point I had worked in advertising, public relations, and marketing. I had also been the associate registrar of a college, but none of the jobs I had held up to that point had really excited me. I wanted to do something I really cared about.

I've always loved to write and I've had a lifelong interest in alternative ways of thinking, scientific anomalies, and unexplainable phenomena. With these things in mind, I decided to approach the owners of a local holistic health magazine, Jeff and Diana Krauth, to talk them into hiring me. It took some doing, but eventually they asked me to be the editor of the magazine they had started in 1979 called *Many Hands*. The name comes from the expression 'Many hands make light work,' and the magazine contained a listing of all the local holistic health practitioners including psychotherapists, astrologers, acupuncturists, massage therapists, bodyworkers, and many more.

Today there are hundreds of these magazines all over the country, but at that time there were very few. *Many Hands* was one of the first and remains a vital magazine to this day. I was thrilled for the opportunity to edit it, and a year later, I bought it from the owners and published it until September of 2005.

As the publisher, I did virtually all of the tasks involved in producing the magazine which included selling the ads that supported it; choosing and editing the articles; designing the layout; choosing the graphics; developing distribution sites; and sometimes even driving around New England to distribute it myself. I also produced the flats (large paper boards with each page of the magazine pasted down on them), which I took to the printer for the final printed edition. In those days everything was done by hand; there was no way to send PDF files electronically.

Over the course of time I hired a friend to do some typing and to help me with the editing, which freed me up to focus on the sales, and to expand the magazine's reach and volume. She was a wonderful help to me, but years later she moved away. By then computers and software had improved to the point where producing the magazine single-handedly again was much more manageable. Then in January of 2005, I gave a workshop on marketing at the Central Massachusetts School of Massage Therapy and realized I had a lot to say about how to run a small business. My original energy for producing the magazine had run its course, and I was very happy when the local newspaper, the *Daily Hampshire Gazette,* agreed to buy it and infuse it with new, creative energy, using all the resources available to a newspaper.

What I experienced over the years through my clients is what prompts me to write this book. I spent hours on the phone with people answering questions, making suggestions, working on their ad copy, and advising them on presentations. I observed that the people who paid on time were also the people who were getting clients. I decided to look at that more carefully because it was not immediately obvious to me why there should be a connection between the two. I started a more systematic study of who was doing well and who was not, and why. I looked at a variety of offices. I went through my billing for late payments, and determined how many of my original clients were still in business, and how many had gone under. I realized that too many holistic practitioners do not have any business training, and that such training is not just a matter of common sense, as some people might think. So I decided to put my own knowledge of the subject into this book as a guide.

I care about what happens to holistic practitioners because I know how important they are to our society. As I mentioned earlier, I've fielded dozens of calls from extremely grateful people all over New England who have told me they would not have been cured, or their condition would not have improved, if they had not had access to the holistic health practitioners that appeared in *Many Hands*. But, believe it or not, although I heard this for many years, I had not had a holistic healing experience myself. Then one day when playing badminton, I tilted my head back too far, and suffered a very stiff neck. I thought it would go away by itself, but six weeks later when the pain was still there, I went to my first chiropractor. Within minutes of his manipulation of my neck, the pain was gone and has never returned, but I have returned to him many times since for other ailments and injuries.

More recently, a member of my family went through a year of physical trauma, going from doctor to doctor, without finding relief for a chronic infection. The doctors were very well-meaning, tried everything they could think of, but remained totally baffled by the continuing problem. I sent this relative to my homeopath and within a month, the condition had completely cleared up. Even *I* was surprised, but since then I have had no doubts about the potential benefits that holistic practitioners have to offer us.

I can't say enough good things about the people I've worked with through the magazine, and it makes me very sad to know that some of them are not succeeding. Holistic health practitioners are a wonderful, soulful, sensitive group of people who in many ways represent the best of humanity through their caring natures. If you are such a practitioner, you know what I'm talking about. In my experience, most practitioners are more than willing to help friends, neighbors, and family members; but are too often unsophisticated in the ways of the marketplace. They need a little guidance in an area that, for the most part, is foreign to them. Using language they understand instead of technical business jargon, I hope to guide them through some very easy steps that, if followed, should lead to the fulfillment they were hoping for when they began their training as a practitioner. The world needs to see many more holistic practitioners out there.

CHAPTER ONE

Certified or Licensed— Okay, Now What?

Did you know that 60% of acupuncturists see fewer than 30 patients weekly? In the same poll, 58% reported that their acupuncture practice is their sole source of income and 40% earned less than $30,000. Massage therapists are suffering the same fate with an attrition rate of some 50,000 graduates leaving the profession every year, according to the Associated Bodywork and Massage Professionals (ABMP). Why the low rate of return for such promising professions? Why do some practitioners fail two years out of school while others succeed year after year? Answer: a simple lack of business skills.

Some Statistics for Thought

As we know, the holistic health industry and all areas of alternative health care have grown exponentially in the last ten years and continue to do so. Exciting success stories about people who have found relief from their ailments by going to homeopaths, acupuncturists or hypnotherapists are legion. People throughout the country are seeking relief for a variety of lingering ailments such as tendonitis, bursitis and back pain—ailments hard to treat successfully with traditional Western medical techniques—and doctors are prescribing massage for patients with chronic pain and stiffness. Both the need for help when traditional medicine fails, and the rising cost of health care, have prompted many people to seek alternative modalities.

So we know the numbers of practitioners are increasing rapidly even though getting exact figures is difficult because certifying boards use different standards to keep statistics. According to the most recent study of the National Institute of Health, 36 percent of American adults use some form of Complementary and Alternative Medicine (CAM). The largest percentage go for treatment of musculoskeletal conditions or chronic pain, thus the increase in the number of massage therapists, chiropractors and bodyworkers. For example, the National Certification Board of Therapeutic Massage and Bodyworkers has been inundated with applications for enrollment. The American Association of Oriental Bodyworkers alone lists over 20,000 licensed acupuncturists in this country today and these are only two of the ninety-plus holistic therapies.

Here are some examples of how rapidly and how much the alternative health care picture is changing. The list at the end of this chapter will give you an idea of how many and how diverse alternative therapies are.

- According to a timeline created by www.wholehealthnow.com, by the mid 1970s there were fewer than 100 physicians who specialized in homeopathy in the United States, and an estimated 1,000 physicians specializing in homeopathy by the mid-1980s, so the number of homeopaths had multiplied by ten in a decade.
- If we count M.D.s, naturopaths, osteopaths, chiropractic physicians, and homeopaths, the number approaches tens of thousands today.
- According to the National Center for Homeopathy there are four accredited medical colleges of naturopathic medicine and each of these teaches a full curriculum in homeopathic medicine. There are approximately another dozen homeopathic schools that teach homeopathy to a wide audience of other health professionals who use homeopathic medicines including dentists, veterinarians, physician

assistants, nurses, acupuncturists, chiropractors, and psychologists, thus increasing dramatically the number of people employing homeopathic medicine in their practices.

With so much demand for services, it's a downright shame that novice practitioners are giving up when they are not able to make ends meet. We need to fix that.

Get A Grip on "Holistic!"

Most likely you're reading this book because you *are* a holistic practitioner, so take heart. Help is on the way and it won't be as difficult to get going in the right direction as you might think.

But before we go any further, we have to backtrack just a little. It's really important for you to know where the term "holistic" comes from, not only because it is used frequently in your profession, but because the concept is one you will need to apply to your business as well. The word was coined to refer to an emerging medical practice that takes into account the whole person—not just the physical parts, but the emotional, spiritual and mental aspects as well. The word has also appeared as "wholistic," which is closer to the word "whole," but now is most often seen as "holistic," which is closer to "holy." Some practitioners feel more of a kinship with the latter because the notion that the healer enables the patient to heal him or herself is also a way of expressing the spiritual idea that the healer helps reveal the divine being within—that healing is a holy practice. Concepts such as these began to take hold in the United States when the spiritual traditions of yoga and Buddhism from central Asia and the Far East became popular in the 1960s.

For years, most of western allopathic (traditional) medicine eschewed the medical practices of the previous 5,000 or so years in favor of methods thought to represent a more scientific approach. Ancient ways that included poultices made of herbs, the use of flower essences, color stimulation, gentle cranial manipulation, and meditation for the purpose of healing, were regarded as backward and in some cases, possibly even harmful. There was a perception that practices from the past were based on superstition and ignorance.

In the twentieth century, the scientific medical model was regarded as miraculous when pharmaceutical companies were able to produce drugs and vaccines that virtually eliminated typhoid, cholera, small pox, malaria, tuberculosis, and eventually polio. People unfortunate enough to contract virulent pneumonia had a high rate of survival thanks to penicillin. Quarantines virtually disappeared. It is not hard to understand why the American public, and much of the civilized world, embraced drug therapy as a panacea. In addition, surgical procedures continued to improve in all areas.

At about the time that interest in Chinese, Japanese, Ayurvedic, and Native American medicine was beginning to grow, it was becoming more evident in traditional medical circles that the heavy hit from a pharmaceutical offering quick relief from illness, often resulted in a negative side effect later on. It was determined that too many antibiotics, for example, could eventually render a patient immune to the drugs if taken too often, and thus vulnerable to disease. In addition, patients who were not getting the help they hoped to receive from the allopathic community started to look into alternative care which offered the promise of slower, but more effective treatment in the end.

In our country, we've gone from house calls by the doctor in the 1950s to describing our complaints very briefly in the doctor's office today. What many of us have come to regard as a typical visit to the doctor might be a scenario like this one: a patient shows up red-faced, complaining of chest pains and anxiety. The doctor performs the usual tests for heart strength and blood pressure, writes a prescription for medication, and sends the patient out the door. Doctors in this instance are often criticized for not taking enough time to acknowledge the patient; to listen to his or her real needs; and for scheduling so many patients back to back that they have no choice but to shoo them out unceremoniously to get through their schedule for the day. Worse, the doctor may not remember the patient the next time that person returns to the office. This lack of a personal touch has driven many people away from traditional practices, especially if they are battling a mysterious or persistent illness.

As a result, the last decades of the 20th century witnessed the steady growth of "alternative" or "holistic" healthcare, as patients rightfully demanded more of their healer's time and attention. For a while there was a total division between the two: holistic (no drugs; surgery in emergencies only) versus allopathic (only drugs and surgery). This division was ridiculously narrow and confusing. A torn meniscus, for example, cannot be repaired with herbs. Should people have to hobble forever after that one tennis game just because the injury wasn't life threatening? On the other hand, is the steady ingestion of drugs the best method of managing health? To reconcile these issues, eventually additional terms emerged such as "complementary" and "integrative" health to include the importance of both kinds of care, and ultimately *all* kinds of care.

For the purposes of this book, "holistic" refers to the comprehensive health care of the individual patient. The business practices described are designed to accommodate the needs of holistic practitioners from a wide range of practices (despite my frequent reference to massage therapists), but they can also be useful to small business owners of any kind.

Ready, Set, Roll! Running a Business

If you are a bodyworker, counselor, or otherwise holistic health practitioner, you've already made your decision to soothe the bodies, minds, and spirits of the many people seeking your help. Either you have graduated from an accredited school or are about to enroll in the school of your choice. In either case, your education about running a business may have just begun. Whether you are a sole proprietor, partner, or corporation, there are things you need to know about making your new career a lasting one.

Let's say you've just received certification and/or a license to practice your craft. In a sense you have chosen a dual career in the same way an artist does. Artists start out by spending long hours in their studios developing techniques, playing with different shades of light and color, and honing their skills to the point where they are ready to show their work, and finally make some money. Here comes their second job: marketing their work.

Marketing might not have been a feature of what the artist loved about creating art in the first place. In fact, he or she may not have even considered what is involved in getting into a juried show, pricing pieces, putting together an installation, or soliciting both patrons and buyers. To many artists at that point, it may seem like a monumental job—one for which they are ill prepared and one that weighs them down.

But it doesn't have to be that way. Running a business requires very different skills than counseling or working with one's hands, as I've learned from talking to hundreds of practitioners. Fortunately that doesn't have to be an impediment for those with no experience. There are some very specific steps that can be followed to make critical business details less of a hassle.

Given the demand for your services, you might think that all you need to do now that you have your certification is hang out your shingle and watch the line to your office form. Unfortunately, it's not quite that easy. There are several things you need to do first. This book will provide an easy guide for you to follow and show you some ways you can differentiate your practice from that of others. Here are some of the things you will discover in the subsequent chapters.

First, I will show you the preliminary steps involved in organizing your business. Do you have systems in place for billing clients, and recording and developing leads for new clients? Have you decided what kind of service or mechanism you will use to answer your phone when you are not available? How will you schedule appointments? Have you thought about a sliding fee scale and how, or to whom, you would apply it? What does your office look like? Does it represent you? Do you have a reliable sound system for playing background music? To successfully run your business having answers to these questions is critical, so first we will address all the details of setting up your office, business, and financial systems. You will no doubt want to spend your time improving the techniques of your profession, learning new methods, and keeping up with current developments in your field—not on the nitty-gritty day-to-day details. Finding a way to make those details a very small but efficient part of your day will give you the extra time you need for the other things you want to be doing.

After you have successfully lined up your office procedures, you will need to advertise. Perhaps you have a lot of friends and relatives who want to avail themselves of your services. That's great for starters, but for a practice to continue with a steady stream of clients for years and years, you need to seek clients from a wider circle. Word of mouth is good, but a strategic advertising campaign is better and the results may last longer.

Before you create that first advertisement, however, you need to be ready. Like a diver at an important meet, you need substantial practice before plunging into the pool. You want to be confident you have covered all the bases so that when you see your first ad in a newspaper or a magazine, you can smile with satisfaction knowing you are ready for your first client to walk in the door. I will show you how to determine who you are in business, what kind of clients you want, what fee to charge, and how to present yourself and your business to the general public. I will also show you how to create your own advertisement and I will make recommendations about where and how you should advertise, and how to promote your business in small ways every day.

Finally, you will learn how to take care of yourself in order to prevent burnout. You will learn techniques for replenishing your energy so that you can look forward to each day of work knowing that you are prepared to handle whatever comes your way.

Holistic Practices (See Glossary for Definitions)

Acupuncture
Acupressure
Asian Medicine & Therapies
Alexander Technique
Apitherapy
Aquatic Bodywork
Applied Kinesiology
Alternative Medicine & Therapies
Aromatherapy

Art, Dance & Music Therapy
Ayurvedic Medicine
Biofeedback
Biological Dentistry
Bodywork Therapies
Bowen Therapy
Breema
Buteyko
Chelation Therapy
Chinese Medicine & Therapies
Chiropractic Care
Colon Therapy
Color Therapy (Chromotherapy)
Craniosacral Therapy
Dietary Therapy
Energy Medicine
Environmental Medicine
Enzyme Therapy
Fasting Therapies
Feldenkrais
Feng Shui
Flower Essences
Folk Medicine
Guided Imagery
Gemstone Therapy
Geriatric Massage
Hakomi
Hellerwork
Herbal Medicine
Holistic Dentistry
Holistic Medicine
Homeopathy
Hydrotherapy
Hyperthermia Therapies
Hypnotherapy
Huna

Infant Massage
Iridology
Juice Therapy
Light Therapy (Phototherapy)
Lomi Lomi
Macrobiotics
Magnetic Field Therapy
Massage Therapy
Medical Massage
Meditation
Mind/Body Medicine
Myotherapy
Natural Food Therapies
Physiotherapy
Naturopathic Medicine
Naprapathy
Neural Therapy
Neuro-Linguistic Programming
Neuromuscular Therapy (NMT)
Nutritional Supplement Therapy
Oriental Bodywork
Ortho-Bionomy
Orthomolecular Medicine
Osteopathic Medicine
Oxygen Therapy
Polarity Therapy
Pranic Healing
Qigong
Reflexology
Reiki
Rosen Method
Rubenfeld
Sclerology
Shen Therapy
Shiatsu
Somatic Education

Sound Therapy
Structural Integration
T'ai Chi
Thai Massage
Therapeutic Touch
Tibetan Medicine
Trepanation
Tui Na
Yoga

Summary

It's important to know the historical background of the alternative or holistic movement. You'll want to apply the same thoroughness to your business that you apply to all aspects of your individual client's health. Doing so requires thinking about a lot of details as you set up your practice, but if you follow my instructions for organizing your practice, these details will become a small part of your daily routine and will not overwhelm you. Many different types of practices, or modalities, will benefit from the guide that follows because all small businesses have more things in common than aspects that differ.

CHAPTER TWO

Start Smart!

Spice Up Your Business Plan

Most likely you'll have had some training in school for filing a business plan in order to secure a loan from a bank, but we're going to go over ways to add some kick to your plan. Banks want to know whether or not you have given the right amount of consideration to the details of your future business. A good business plan will serve as an excellent outline for helping you identify and answer some of the questions a bank will be asking.

Business plan forms are readily available through libraries, the Internet, colleges, banks, and lending institutions, but you can create your own. The forms themselves may vary, but there are basically seven standard components to a business plan. These components may be called by different names as you can see below. This can be very confusing, but understand that the basic functions of each category are the same on all business plans.

1. **Introduction or Introductory Contents:** This includes a cover page with your contact information, and an Executive Summary, which is one of the most important aspects of a business plan. It may also be called the Overview, the Owner's Statement, the Concept, or the Business Summary depending on what form you choose to use.

2. Business Description or The Objective: This is a description of the company and its product(s) or service(s).

3. The Market; Market Analysis; or Market Strategies: What the lender is looking for here is whether you have done any research to see if there is really room for your business in the current market. What conclusions have you drawn from this research?

4. Competitive Analysis; Production; or Development and Production: This category should cover how your product is created, or how your service will be carried out. It should include equipment; sources and costs of materials; and the cost of facilities. Keep it to a minimum figure.

5. Design and Development Plan; Marketing; or Sales and Marketing: Use this section to describe how you plan to bring in clients and expand your business.

6. Management; Organization and People; or Operations and Management Plan: This is where, as a sole proprietor, you want to describe the reasons why you will be a good risk. What qualifies you for this business? Bankers know that successful small businesses depend greatly on the person running the show. Don't hesitate to toot your own horn here!

7. Financial Documents; Financial Components; or Financial Projections: This section is where you divulge the amount of money you are hoping to obtain, and how it will be disbursed. Include current investments (if any) and your projected annual income.

People applying for business loans often make the mistake of starting out with the last section first, asking for money right off the bat. Instead, we're going to go back and address the Executive Summary in a little more detail, because this is the first thing most lenders look for and read. It's the section that can either make them sit up and take notice, or decide your business is not worthy of their investment. This is your chance to "wow" the bank with your unique approach to your profession. This process may seem intimidating, but remember that you know your craft better than the banker does.

Use terms that are understandable, but that also reflect your professional knowledge.

One way to isolate your individuality and add a needed kick to your Executive Summary is to think about what brought you to your profession in the first place. Susan, for example, wants to open a massage therapy office. She has received her license, and looks (on paper) like many other massage therapists. The bank only has so much money to lend to female small business owners. How will they decide to choose her over someone else? Susan explains that she intends to specialize in infant massage because she witnessed the importance of this specialty when her nephew developed a problem in the hospital. The mother was very concerned about the possible effects of surgery or drugs on such a small child. Several sessions with an infant massage therapist solved the problem, negating the need for drugs or surgery in his case. Susan was impressed with how quickly a non-invasive procedure could work, and is determined to use her skills to help other children and their parents in this way.

EXERCISE

Imagine that you are standing in a line of your friends who are being asked one by one to step forward and tell their own story. Is there something you can say about yourself that will not be true for anyone else in that line? Use it. Figure out a way to incorporate it in your business plan. Take time with this particular piece. It will become an invaluable part of your business, and you will employ it again and again.

If you are not confident about filling out a business plan, or writing one of your own, it's a good idea to have a professional writer or an established business person review your plan before you submit it to a bank or loan source.

For more information about filling out a business plan, see the list of agencies in Appendix A that are available to help small businesses. One of the most helpful is SCORE (Service Corps of Retired Executives), an organization of retired business professionals with over 380 chapters across the country, who donate their time and energy free of charge to people just starting out in business. These are people who truly want to help you get going, and are often more accessible than government agencies or private business people. The headquarters for SCORE is located in Washington, D.C., the phone number is 800/634-0245, and the email address is www.score.org.

About Business Loans

Business loans fall into four basic categories: fixed rate loans; adjustable rate or floating rate loans; secured loans; and unsecured loans. Fixed rate loans will have one interest rate for the duration of the repayment period, whereas adjustable or floating rate loans will have higher interest rates imposed as the repayment period progresses based on changes in the market and in government policies regarding interest rates. Recently adjustable/floating rate loans have received a lot of bad press as foreclosures abound. People who took out this kind of loan found that several years down the road they were unable to pay the inevitably higher rates. A fixed rate loan is preferable if you can get one, because it allows you to know exactly how much you can expect to pay on a monthly basis for the entire length of the loan.

A secured loan requires some kind of collateral, like property or savings, which the bank can take from you if you fail to repay the loan. In the case of an unsecured loan, there is no requirement for collateral, but these loans often have very high interest rates. You want to make sure that whomever you're borrowing money from, the source is a legitimate one, such as a bank with a national reputation, or the government.

The government supplies small business loans through the Small Business Administration (SBA) for all kinds of businesses including holistic health practices. Factors you'll want to take into account before securing a loan, many of which appear throughout this book, include the monthly repayment costs. As you go read along, keep the figures below in mind knowing that they will be a starting point. These figures are for *unsecured* loans only, and do not include processing fees or state taxes, but they will give you a general idea of what you can expect to pay monthly at 12.5% interest over three, four, and five-year loan periods. The banking industry refers to these tables as the amortization of a loan.

For a $30,000 loan, the monthly costs would be $1,114, $806, or $682.

For a $40,000 loan, the monthly cost would be $1,350, $1,072, or $908.

For a $50,000 loan, the monthly cost would be $1,685, $1,339, or $1,135.

Setting Goals for Your Business

As you put the finishing details on your business plan, let your mind begin to drift into the future. What do you hope to achieve with your business? What are your plans for making those achievements reality? If you never take the time to establish goals, you may find yourself spinning around in a circle. Goals help you move forward since they are things you're reaching for; you have to move from point A to Point B to achieve them. You have to take action.

Writing your goals down is a powerful way to make them actually happen. As with positive affirmations that you repeat to yourself, written goals can help spur you along at times when your energy relative to your business may be dragging. Place your written goals in a drawer and pull them out to read periodically. Maybe at that point you will think, "Oops, I haven't done anything to achieve *that* goal—better get started." Or, you may decide that one of the original goals you set for yourself is no longer relevant and needs to be revised. Add some new ones.

In order to be successful in business, you have to be a planner. You have to think ahead—to anticipate problems and challenges—while at the same time acknowledging significant benchmarks along the way. Goal setting is an easy way to foster this process. If it doesn't come naturally to you, start slowly and build up to it. Eventually you'll discover that planning ahead and setting goals for yourself will save you an enormous amount of hardship later on. If you don't know how to begin this process, here's an easy exercise. Let's say for the sake of argument, you're in your mid-twenties. Take a minute to imagine your life for the next forty years in a thumbnail sketch. It's tough, I know, but just try it. It might go something like this:

"I graduate from acupuncture school, get married, open an office, struggle along for the first few years, have children, see more clients, build the practice, learn new techniques, start to slow down, and retire."

It doesn't sound all that appealing does it? Yet this is how most of the world approaches life—we may take initial action, but we just let the rest of life happen to us, coping and adjusting when necessary. What if you were to describe it differently right from the start?

"I graduate from acupuncture school, find a wonderful spouse or partner, open a spectacular office, plan carefully for the first few years and watch that planning pay off with excellent results, have two phenomenal children, become well known in my field, start to slow down while imparting my knowledge to a new generation, and retire to the island of my choice with more than enough money to enjoy my later years."

The difference is the anticipation of a wonderful future. How can you have one if you don't *plan* on having one? Your life as a business owner will always be influenced by factors outside your control, but if you stop to think about how you might handle every single aspect of your life with a goal for each one, and are clear about how you are going to achieve those goals, you have a road map for success. You may have to take a detour from time to time, but at least you've developed a valuable reference tool.

Think about how your personal life is likely to intersect with your business life. Take time with your family to make sure your goals are all in sync. If not, what can you do to achieve more of a consensus? As you move through this guide, learning about expenses, fees, and many other things, you'll be able to define each one of your goals more distinctly. For now, just read the following list of questions and try to keep them in mind as you go:

1. What is the purpose of my business?

2. How can I attract the clients I want?

3. What will help me derive overall satisfaction from my practice?

4. What do I need to make in annual income?

5. Where do I want to be in one year, in three years, and in five years?

6. How can I successfully coordinate my family and social life with my business schedule?

7. What do I want to achieve as a parent, spouse or partner?

8. What are the top priorities of my life?

As you can imagine, this list can get quite long. Start with the basics and jot down any others that come to mind. The more subject matter you can come up with, the more you can "flesh out" your dream. Use all your senses to support your process. Make your own audiotape, or dictate a message for your iPod that reminds you periodically of where you want your life compass to direct you. Put up a visual reminder somewhere you are likely to see it every day. Keep a small, smooth stone in your pocket and when you're waiting in line at the grocery store, or for a plane at the airport, rub the stone with your fingers and use an affirmation like, "My life is proceeding very smoothly," to reinforce this idea. Keep doing it and you'll find that it works. These techniques are nothing more than positive reinforcement for a plan you devised for yourself. The more positive energy you put into your plan, the sooner it is likely to materialize.

Where Should You Begin Your Practice?

Assuming you have secured your loan and set goals for your business, the next step is to determine where you want to practice. If you are as free as a bird and can go anywhere, you'll want to do some research on the various areas of the country, or the world, that appeal to you. If you are like most of us, however, you already know where you want to practice because you are tied to a spouse, a partner, children, parents, relatives, or friends.

Speaking of family, it's a good idea to have a serious talk with your family members about what they can expect of your business in terms of its demands on your time. Prepare them for the fact that even though you'll have more flexibility in your schedule now that you're working for yourself, you probably won't have more free time overall. The truth is most business owners work many more hours than the normal 40-hour workweek. This time often does not seem so burdensome, however, since you're not under the thumb of a boss, but it can still amount to a lot of time away from home and family. This is especially true when you're first starting out and trying to establish a regular clientele.

Try to incorporate family members in your routine, if possible, so as to make them a part of your new project. Small children for example, might love the opportunity to go to your office with you on a weekend and "help" clean. Factoring time into your day for your partner or spouse will nip trouble in the bud, even if it's just for half an hour. The people who love you don't want to feel excluded from your now very busy life. If you include them from the beginning, you're likely to get more cooperation from them over the long haul.

Legal Issues

The process of setting up a business is more circular—even spherical—than it is linear or chronological. I've tried to lay it out in as straightforward and logical a manner as I could, but it's a challenging process. For example, before you can bring in clients, you have to have an office. Before you can rent an office, you have to know how much money you'll be bringing in and what kind of rent you can afford. Before you know how much money you'll be bringing in, you have to set your fee, and so it goes. Be patient. We are going to cover all these things. This book is set up so that you can read it through once to get the overall gist of running a business, and then use it as a guide by going back to particular chapters for technical or more specific information. You don't have to know everything by heart by the time you finish reading it.

I'm addressing the legal issues you face first because they are so important to the protection of your business. Securing your legal status as a practitioner can take more time than you might like, but without a strong legal foundation for your practice, everything else could prove futile. Checking into the various statutes relevant to your practice can be boring and tedious, but knowing them is so essential, there is no reason to begin elsewhere. If you have never had to research the law before, this chapter will at least alert you to what you need to know, and how you can obtain the information. As a business owner, you'll have to do this on a regular basis to stay in good standing with your state, county, city and community.

State Laws

No matter where you decide to practice, you will want to check the state laws to see if your particular profession is legal and regulated and, if so, what the requirements and restrictions are. If you are registered with the state, do you also need to be certified? If you have certification, do you also need a license? Be aware that the terminology can be very confusing and needs to be interpreted carefully. Just recently, Colorado made changes to its laws regarding acupuncture that required registration with the state. Even though the *process* of registering with this state will remain the same with the new legislation, the *name* of the process has been changed from "registration" to "licensure."

In the case of acupuncture, for example, statutes making acupuncture legal have varied widely among the states. Acupuncturists in Vermont were allowed to practice legally with only certification beginning in 1994. Then in 1997, they were required to obtain a license. However, New Hampshire, Vermont's next-door neighbor, didn't even legalize acupuncture until 1997.

Currently there appear to be 35 states that have legal statutes on the books for acupuncturists, but that number can be deceiving because new legislation is introduced all the time, and because individual states have different reporting procedures that may or may not produce exact numbers of licensed acupuncturists in that state. For example, there are many physicians (MDs) who are allowed to practice acupuncture under certain conditions, but who may not have an actual license for acupuncture. In addition, requirements vary from state to state in terms of how many hours of training are needed for licensure and what kind of educational requirements are necessary.

Another wrinkle is the growing number of practitioners who combine different modalities, like a homeopath who also practices acupuncture. In Nevada, homeopaths may practice acupuncture within certain statutes and regulations, but may not "practice, advertise or utilize acupuncture" beyond those very specific statutes. In this case the state legislature of Nevada is recognizing that acupuncture is a complex method of healing that requires rigorous training and that certain aspects of it should only be performed by a licensed acupuncturist.

These examples are offered to reinforce the idea that before you do anything else, you must understand the laws of your state regarding your practice. And, you must keep up with these statutes and regulations because they change frequently. There are many ways to track down this information starting with your local reference librarian or the Internet. If it is not clear how recent the information on the Internet is, find a phone number for the certifying body in your state and call to make sure your information is up to date.

Make a note to yourself to check this information on a regular six-month basis. If you have trouble understanding the language, hire a lawyer to help you. We will talk more about lawyers later on, but this is an instance where an understanding of the meaning of the law is paramount. You don't want to go to the trouble of setting up a practice only to discover you are not operating legally. You can often work out a fee with a lawyer for a half hour phone call just to get some quick answers to your legal concerns once your business moves along.

Zoning Restrictions and City Registrations

In addition to state laws, there may be zoning restrictions; and city regulations and ordinances that you need to know. For example, do zoning laws allow you to operate out of your house? Some cities require a zoning permit in addition to simple compliance with the law. In such cases you are required to have an inspection by the city inspector. Once you have been approved, you must post this permit somewhere in your office. The traditional zones of a city are recognized as agricultural, residential, commercial and industrial. The advent of telecommuting, and more people working from home on their computers, has blurred the distinction between residential and commercial. Even the IRS has relaxed some of its restrictions along these lines in terms of claiming a home office, but it is still important that you know the laws of your city.

Almost every city will want you to register your business for tax purposes. Whether you operate out of your house or out of an office, it is illegal not to declare your business status and the penalties for failing to do so can vary widely. If operating illegally, you may have to pay back taxes and perhaps have your business closed down. Most city taxes on small businesses do not amount to much financially and are well worth paying for your peace of mind. If you are not sure about the zoning laws in your city, your Chamber of Commerce can tell you where to find out what they are. There may also be a Business Licensing Commission or Bureau, but the Chamber people will know where to direct you. City regulations vary quite a bit. Some require special licensing in addition to obtaining a business license and some even require fingerprinting.

You may also need to check the laws regarding business signs, known as "signage." How large a sign can you put up for your business and how far away from the curb must it be? All of these things are carefully regulated in many cities and states. Just be aware that virtually every aspect of running your business will have implications at the city, state, and perhaps township level in terms of the law and taxes.

Permits

Since we're on the subject of legalities, here is another area that needs to be addressed so that you can sleep soundly at night: permits. Sometimes you will need to receive an actual license or permit from the city in addition to simply registering. Some cities require an occupational license, which is a license recognized by your particular profession, indicating that you are a member in good standing and that your practice complies with their regulations. Whether you are renting or leasing from a landlord, or own the building in which you are practicing, you should know that any changes to the building require a building permit that must be obtained from the building inspector and prominently displayed on or in the building.

Taxes

The three most common types of legal business arrangements are sole proprietorships, partnerships, and corporations. Less common are S corporations that are exempt from some federal taxes, and limited liability companies (LLCs), which limit the liability of its members for debts or losses, and are more like a partnership. The overwhelming majority of holistic practitioners start out as sole proprietors, and many will remain so until they retire. As a sole proprietor, you can deduct many expenses related to the cost of doing business, which means that your taxable income will be less. On the other hand, because you have no employer taking social security and other taxes out of your paycheck on a regular basis, you'll most likely be required to pay quarterly taxes in anticipation of your annual tax debt. This means that you will have to set aside some of that hard-earned income to send to the federal, and possibly the state, government every three months. In addition, if you have not calculated your taxes correctly throughout the year, you may have to pay an additional amount on April 15th of each year.

Business taxes can be complicated. It is worth every penny to hire a good certified public accountant (CPA). You want someone with whom you feel comfortable—someone who is professional, discreet, and able to advance your business. Shop around. Ask other business people whom they would recommend and check with your Chamber of Commerce for reputable CPAs. You may spend more time with this person than you expect to so it is important to have a good working relationship. As with lawyers, you can often work out a fee with an accountant for a half hour phone call of advice. CPAs will know about deductions you might never have thought of like the depreciation of your office equipment, and how to handle barter and in-kind payments. In the end this service will save you money.

I offer a cautionary note here. It is illegal in any state to fail to report any money that comes to you in any form—cash, checks, money orders, bank transfers, paypal, etc. This applies to money from clients, friends and family, even if it is a gift. Legal deductions from taxable income are less clearly defined. You might, for example, receive $50,000 a year in income, but incur $20,000 in legal business deductions for a taxable income of $30,000. Nonetheless you must still report every penny of the $50,000.

Save any business related receipt for seven years. Always dispose of any financial paperwork by shredding it completely. Also, find out if it is necessary for you to charge sales tax for your services in your state. There will undoubtedly be paperwork attached to a sales tax charge, so check with your accountant and find out how much to charge, and how to handle the reporting of these charges.

The IRS website (irs.gov) offers a wealth of information about small businesses, and is more user-friendly than many other sites loaded with technical information. There you can find information about the tax forms you'll need to file such as a Schedule SE for social security self-employment tax; a Schedule C for sole proprietorship profit and loss; and a Form 1040 for your individual tax return. At first, you will go to your accountant for filing these forms, but it is a good idea to familiarize yourself with the types of forms and the concepts behind them because eventually you may want to do this yourself.

Types of Insurance

If you are working on other people's bodies or minds, you need several different types of insurance. Insurance policies can be very tricky to interpret so if you have any doubt about what you are signing up for, consult a lawyer. This is *not* an area you want to gloss over. I once took out an insurance policy for an event I was producing in a hotel. I talked to my insurance agent at some length before I signed the policy and thought that I was insured if there was any damage to the hotel as a result of this event. Unfortunately, days after the event was over, the hotel complained that some of my exhibitors had torn its very expensive wallpaper and wanted reimbursement. I checked with my insurance agent, expecting my insurance company to pay for the damage, but was informed that the policy I had taken out covered every part of the hotel *except* the rooms in which my event took place. It was very disheartening and since then I have conferred with my lawyer on any policies I'm considering.

For each type of insurance, you will need to ask several questions. First, what kind of policy do you really need? As you will see, there are many different kinds of insurance, so be sure you are covered by the appropriate vehicle. Second, how much money do you need to be insured for with each policy, and what is the deductible? Third, where can you get the best deal? Do some comparison-shopping. If you go to only one agent, he or she may be required to represent only a handful of companies that offer that type of insurance. Investigate any kind of group policies you might be eligible for such as coverage offered to alumni of your college, or members of your professional association.

It's possible to save money on insurance premiums by investing in alarm systems, certain types of locks, and other products and procedures recognized by the insurance industry as reducing the risk of you filing a claim for payment. You might also save money by paying premiums on an annual basis instead of monthly or quarterly, or by purchasing several different kinds of insurance from the same company. Don't be afraid to ask questions or make deals. If you have any reservations about the insurance company, check it out with your state insurance commission.

Certain types of insurance are a must for business owners. The actual names of the individual insurances may vary from insurance company to insurance company, and the terminology may also vary, so pay particular attention to what your policy actually covers. Insurance salespeople use their own language that includes terms like "coverage provisions, terms and conditions, policy exclusions, and limits." Ask them to explain what these terms mean in a way you are sure you understand.

In determining how much insurance a company is willing to give you, insurance companies will assess the severity and frequency of losses that you might incur. The higher your risk, the higher the premium is likely to be. Are you likely to get sued frequently by clients who are unhappy with your services, or is this a very small possibility? Is the equipment you use expensive and therefore subject to theft? An insurance agent will ask you questions regarding your qualifications as a practitioner, how long you have been in business, your financial background including any liquid assets, and what kind of products you plan to sell in your practice. Most likely there will be an industry standard for your particular form of therapy, and the insurance agent will adjust that premium figure based on the answers you provide.

One thing to remember about lawsuits as they relate to insurance claims is that intention is a huge factor in determining guilt or innocence. If you have clearly taken steps to reduce your risk by having written policies in place, keeping detailed client files, ensuring that all your equipment is working properly, keeping your office and entryway free of debris, etc., making a case against you will be much harder for the opposing lawyer. Toward that end, you want to stay within the guidelines of your profession and not extend yourself into areas where you do not have the appropriate expertise, like a massage therapist offering nutritional advice. You might be able to give wonderful advice, but you are not insured to do so.

It is also a very good idea to discuss with your insurance agent how the process of a suit goes before anything ever crops up. Ask their advice on what you can do to prevent a loss and exactly what you should do if you are ever sued. Your immediate actions after such a complaint has been leveled could make a difference to the outcome. As with most other aspects of business, it's better to know how to handle these situations beforehand.

Liability and Malpractice

You will want to investigate malpractice insurance (also known as professional liability insurance), Errors & Omissions insurance (E&O), general liability insurance, product liability insurance, and even workman's compensation insurance if you have employees.

Malpractice (professional liability) insurance will cover you if someone sues you for what the industry describes as "a loss or damages" due to your negligence or incompetence. Errors and Omissions insurance, often added to malpractice/professional liability, covers you for any errors or omissions made in the course of performing your professional work as it applies to the delivery of your services. You might think you would never need these types of insurance, but believe me; you can't afford that kind of thinking. This is *not* be a time to count on those positive affirmations.

You can probably obtain the best rate for this kind of insurance by going through your professional association. Your premium will be determined by things like whether or not you are licensed (or otherwise certified in your field), whether you're working full or part-time, and by the laws of the state in which you live. For example, if you are a self-employed physical therapist working fulltime in Massachusetts, your premium for one year would be approximately $450.00, according to Healthcare Providers Service Organization, an excellent source of information (www.hpso.com).

General liability insurance is designed to cover primarily bodily injury and property damages that occur on your premises, and costs between $350 and $500 a year. Some policies are even written to include mental anguish as well. If a client trips on the way into your office, and becomes injured as a result, your general liability insurance should cover the cost. Sometimes general liability is covered by the landlord's insurance, but check with your landlord to make sure *whose* insurance policy is responsible for covering *what* in terms of compensation. Get something in writing from your landlord to this effect. You can't settle for someone's word on something this important. If you are not properly insured, you could end up paying for damages out of your own pocket.

Product liability insurance could be important to you if you are distributing or selling products like herbs or aromatherapy oils. It covers you for manufacturer's defects, legal defense costs, safety claims, medical costs, and spoilage costs. Frequently used with product liability insurance is the term "risk transference," which means that the risk of getting sued for a loss is transferred to someone or something (a corporation) else. Because no one wants to be sued, most businesses make sure they engage in as much risk transference as possible. In the case of product liability, this means that you should be able to transfer your risk to the manufacturer of the product. Check with the manufacturer to see if they are properly insured, and ask if you can be added to their policy as a distributor of their product. Product liability is usually tacked on to a general liability policy and the premiums can range between one and ten percent of annual sales of the product, depending on the product's industry.

Workman's compensation insurance would only be necessary if you have additional full-time employees. If you decide to hire a receptionist at some point, you may want to shop around for insurance premiums to cover the cost of any potential injury to him or her. Individual state laws regulate workman's compensation insurance, and most states have workman's compensation funds from which you can draw, but they also allow the purchase of private policies that are more competitive in price, so it pays to look for a bargain. Premiums are generally more expensive for manufacturing companies than for the service industry.

Insurance for the Business

Let's say you've been in business for a few years and suddenly the economy changes, or you run into problems in your own life. In order not to lose the business, you can take out small business insurance which may provide assistance if factors outside of your control begin to have an impact on your cash flow. In addition, disability insurance will cover you if you become ill or disabled. You may receive a full or partial monthly payment depending on your degree of infirmity. As we all know, life happens, so even if you are totally sound and healthy at this moment, that can change at any time. If you are the primary breadwinner in your family, this type of insurance could be of critical support.

Fire and theft insurance will cover any loss of equipment such as computers, bodywork tables, furniture, etc. You will have to weigh the cost of paying a monthly premium against the cost of replacing everything in your office. If your office is a very simple set-up, it might be less expensive to forego this insurance cost. Make sure to keep hard copies of your client files in your house so you can reconstruct them on a new computer if your office goes up in flames.

Insurance for You

If you use your car to make house calls in your practice, you will need to make sure you have full auto insurance coverage, especially for items related to your practice that are damaged in transit. Most importantly, you need medical health insurance. This can be very expensive, especially for the sole proprietor who may not be covered under a spouse's plan, but fortunately more variations of health insurance are becoming available at literally half the cost of former policies. Massachusetts now requires that all residents have health insurance and has requested that insurance companies doing business in this state provide affordable policies.

In all states, there are policies with options covering doctor visits, medical bills, hospitalizations, drug prescriptions, etc. The one thing you should have is catastrophic coverage. You might be able to cover other expenses in the event of an illness, but if you are in a car accident and end up in the hospital, you can rack up $100,000 worth of medical bills in a couple days. The best bets for lower rates are those provided by your professional association. There are also separate companies, such as the National Association for the Self-Employed, that provide access to affordable health insurance.

Other Things You Need to Know

If you are not planning to use your given name as the name of your business, you may need to register the name of your business with the Fictitious Name Registration Board. To find a sample form (for Pennsylvania residents) go to: www.dos.state.pa.us/corps/lib/corps/20/7/311.pdf. You can find a description of the process for your state by asking your search engine for Fictitious Name Registration in XX (fill in your state). The name you choose will be your DBA (doing business as) name. An EIN is your employer identification number. Many sole proprietors use their social security number as their EIN. Check with your accountant and see what he or she advises. If you use your social security number, be especially careful where, and to whom, it goes. Stolen social security numbers are a major source of identity fraud.

You will want to find out how many other people are practicing your profession in your area of interest and what the competition is like. You can do this by calling other practitioners in your field, checking the yellow pages, and by checking with the city to see how many other practitioners have registered. What is the population of your intended city? Is there room for another massage therapist or would it be a struggle to grab your corner of the market? Sometimes you can figure this out by simply calling other practitioners. Ask about their specialties and what kinds of additional features they offer as part of their practice, like the use of a hot tub after a massage. It may turn out that even though there are a fairly large number of practitioners in your area, there are only one or two who do exactly what you do, like specializing in sports massage. You can also change your opportunities for breaking into the market by adding a service or learning a new technique.

If you are new to an area, the cost of housing and office rental space can be readily determined by calling a real estate agent. You can also check ads in the paper for office rental space. Go to see several places, even if the rent is above what you can pay, so that you can get an idea of how much space you can expect to afford. Other indicators of living expenses include the cost of groceries and the state income tax. Some states have no income tax; others have a 5% to 7% tax.

Before deciding on an office space and signing a lease, you'll want to set-up a specific office budget like the one in the next chapter. This will help you determine how much rent you can afford initially.

Summary

After giving careful thought to your business plan, set goals by asking what you hope to achieve with your business and where you want it to take you in the future. It's important to know your state, county, and city laws regarding your practice. You must also be aware of the kinds of insurances you will need to cover unexpected accidents or malpractice issues, and you need to stay on top of your quarterly tax payments to the government.

Two relationships you want to foster are those with your lawyer and your accountant. They can do a great deal to promote the health and well-being of your business, while saving you time and money. Find people you are comfortable with and would not hesitate to call for last minute advice. Finally, evaluate the costs of living in the community you've chosen for your practice.

CHAPTER THREE

Juggling
All the Numbers

This chapter is designed to help you weed through a lot of gobbledy-gook when trying to decide what to include in your office budget. When you begin your practice, your biggest financial decision will be how much you should pay for rent. Along the way you will have many other decisions to make, but the one that will be the most essential to the start of your practice is what to pay for rent, or, whether or not to rent an office at all.

Unfortunately, in order to get to the bottom line on the rent, it's necessary go through a number of other expenses that come into play. There is a lot of information here so my advice to you is to take your time with this chapter. Don't try to digest it all at once. I know you're ready to get going—rent that office space and start fixing it up, but it's a chicken and an egg thing. Before you can do that, you have to know what else you're going to be paying for. The process of sorting all this out is comparable to an untrained pilot facing a million dials on a control panel. It can seem overwhelming at first, but gradually the pilot becomes familiar with the purpose of each dial, and soon is successfully tweaking one and fiddling with another in order to nagivate the plane smoothly. You can do this, too.

In this chapter, I'll help you evaluate your costs, figure out what you need to make on an annual basis, and then what you can afford to pay for rent. Your budget will naturally depend on the type of practice you have, but there are several major categories that are relevant to all types of business. The purpose here is to familiarize you with line items that are likely to appear in your business budget, but understand that *your particular* budget may differ significantly from the line items and figures indicated here. For example, if you are single, own a house, and rent an office space for your business, your annual income will need to cover both your mortgage and the cost of rent. If you are married or partnered, own a house, and rent an office space, it's possible that your spouse or partner's income pays the mortgage, so the primary cost you have to be concerned with is that of rent for your office. Furthermore, whether you are single or married, if you work from your home, rent for an office space will not be a concern for you.

Another example is the cost of health insurance. If you are covered through your spouse or partner's place of work, you will not need to include this line item in your business budget. Likewise, if you don't own a car and can walk to work, then all of the auto expenses listed in this chapter are irrelevant for you. The same applies to supplies, personal expenditures, and many other things listed as budget line items. For this reason, no total figures appear for the various costs involved. It's not possible within the scope of this book to provide you with exact numbers since your indivdual situation could vary so much, but the listings here will help you begin to think about all the ways in which you need to calculate costs. There may be aspects of your business that are not mentioned. Again, the purpose is to alert you to the kinds of costs you need to consider when making your financial decisions.

At the end of this chapter, we'll evaluate what you can actually make in annual income to cover your costs.

Setting Up a Budget

The expenses listed below are the essential costs of your practice. The first list involves those expenses that you are likely to incur initially for setting up your office. The lists that follow include expenses you will incur on a regular monthly, quarterly, and annual basis.

The way to figure out how much money you need annually in order to meet all your payments is to go through each list and estimate its total cost. Go through the items on the monthly list and multiply the total by 12 to get a total for the year. For the quarterly list, you will multiply the total by four to get your figure for the year, and for the annual list, you will not need to multiply anything—just total the numbers that appear under "Annual Costs." Add the total figure for your monthly costs to the total for your quarterly costs, and then add the annual costs to get a grand total for the year.

You don't need to include your initial costs in this total, because hopefully they have been covered by your business plan loan, and I have included the loan repayments as a line item in the monthly costs.

Initial Set-Up Costs (One-time Only)

Computer
Consultant to teach you recordkeeping and how to bill insurance companies
Equipment
Rent: First and last month of lease, plus security deposit

Monthly Costs

The categories in alphabetical order are:
Advertising: flyers and print ads
Auto: insurance, car payments, and gasoline
Bank charges
Cable for TV, Internet, email, high speed modem
Equipment and professional supplies
Health insurance for you
Insurance for the business: general liability, malpractice, etc.
Insurance for your home
Computer software and maintenance
Website retention and maintenance
Loan payments
Office supplies
Parking: if you have to pay to park in a parking garage
Personal/Draw
Phones: office, cell and/or home phone
Postage

Rent for the business
Rent or mortgage for your home
Utilities for the business and for home

Quarterly Costs

Taxes: You will have to pay quarterly taxes.

Annual Costs

Accountant fees
Advertising: brochures and business cards
Auto maintenance
Domain name fee
Dues for your professional organization
Lawyer fees
Licenses and permits
Taxes: any money owed on April 15th after paying quarterly taxes

You'll notice none of these lists includes travel, the cost of taking refresher courses, clothing, entertainment, furniture, decorating, attending trade shows where you might demonstrate your work, or other costs that you will eventually need to cover. We will address some of these at the end of this process. The items listed above are the essentials you want to keep in mind for the purpose of requesting a business loan, and signing a lease for your office. Let's go through each category, and give it a possible dollar figure, but keep in mind these figures are just estimates that may not apply to you.

Advertising (brochures, business cards and print ads):
$50/month; $200 annually

You will probably order 500 business cards and 500 brochures to start since many printing companies require a 500 minimum order. After 500, the unit cost, or the cost of each individual item (business card or brochure), goes up substantially. You probably won't need to print your business cards or brochures more than once a year, which will cost about $200. Placing an advertisement with a regular newspaper or magazine can cost from $30 a month to $200 a month. Let's give this a $50 per month cost to start.

Auto: $550/month; $500 annually

Auto insurance rates vary by state but most likely will cost between $50 and $100/month. Gasoline costs depend on how many miles you drive in a month, but let's say its about $60 to $100 a month. Car payments if you do not own your car can be between $300 and $500 per month.

Bank Charges: $25/month

Bank charges can vary greatly depending on what kind of an account you have. A business checking account will incur maintenance fees of about $20, whereas a personal account will be more like $10, or no cost at all if you do not let the balance fall below a certain amount. If you also have an arrangement for allowing clients to make credit card payments for Visa, Mastercard, Discover, and American Express, there is usually an annual fee for this service of around $200 through the merchant services branch of your bank. In addition, banks ususally charge another fee for each transaction. We'll assume you do not have such an option at the beginning of your practice, but as your business grows you may want to add this feature.

An average figure for this category is going to be $25 a month to start.

Cable: $100/month

The costs of cable depend on how many devices you are using through cable and whether or not you are operating out of your house versus renting an office space. If you are operating from home and have cable for your TV (including high definition), a high speed modem, Internet and email access, you can expect to pay between $50 and $150 a month, depending on how many options you decide to purchase.

If you have an additional cable for your office to use the Internet, the cost will go up by about $50, assuming there is not a TV in your office as well. We'll estimate this item at $100 per month—$60 for home, $40 for office.

Computer and Related Items: $25/month; $1,000 initially

The initial cost of a computer is between $500 and $2,500. We will add it at the end since it's a one-time expense. Here we are going to include the cost of software and possibly computer maintenance and/or consultation if you ever need help from a technician.

Equipment and Professional Supplies:
$150/month; $1,000 initially

If you are a bodyworker and need to replenish your supply of sheets and massage therapy oils, your costs are going to be higher than for a psychotherapist who does not need equipment in the same way. Remember that this figure is an average monthly figure. You may go months without needing new equipment, but then spend $800 one month on a new bodywork table.

Health Insurance Costs: $250/month

Medical insurance payments for the self-employed can run between $200 and $500, depending on the amount of your deductible, with an additional $20 to $25 for a co-payment to see a doctor. If you are covered under your spouse's or partner's policy, you will not have to list this as a business expense.

Insurance: $125/month

Homeowners insurance ranges between $400 to $2,000 a year depending on the assessed value of your home, your deductible, and the type of coverage you have, but let's estimate this at $650 or about $50 a month; malpractice/professional liability insurance runs about $450 a year, or about $37.50 a month, and insurance for the business (general liability) costs between $350 and $500, or about $35 a month. We'll estimate this monthly total at around $125 per month.

Loan Payments: $800/month

These payments will include payments to the bank for your business loan. A business loan for $30,000 at an interest rate of 12.5% paid back over a three-year period, will require an annual repayment of $12,043.32, or a monthly repayment of approximately $1,114. If the repayment period is extended to 5 years, the monthly payment reduces to $682 per month. You may also have a credit card payment to make which I've given an arbitrary figure of $118. (Be sure to pay your credit cards off in full each month so as not to incur a finance charge.) We're going to round this figure out to $800/month.

Office Supplies: $50/month

Office supplies will include any paper products, envelopes, kleenex, stationery items such as staples and rubber bands—virtually anything that you use on a regular basis in your office that does not fall into one of the other categories.

Parking: $50/month

If your office is in an office building, and you have to park in a parking garage, you may incur a monthly fee of between $50 and $100 dollars depending on the location. Obviously, if you do not have to pay to park, you can disregard this category altogether.

Personal Items: $1,000/month

Personal items are things like clothing, entertainment, groceries, and vacations. Another name commonly used for this category is "Draw," that is, the amount of money you draw from your account to cover personal, as opposed to business, expenses. If you entertain clients for the purpose of business, or buy items of clothing that are essential to your practice as in the case of a yoga instructor, you may be able to claim these as business expenses if they are placed in separate categories for "Entertainment" and "Clothing" respectively. If this is the case, subtract these costs from the "Personal" category, and add line items for the new categories.

Phones: $100/month

A cell phone, and/or land lines at the home and the office can add up. To save money you might be able drop one of them (probably your land line at home), but I do not recommend relying on a cell phone for your office business. You don't want to have to cope with dropped calls or dead zones when discussing business with a client. You also don't want people calling you and leaving messages at your home. The cost of one cell, and one land line for the office, will be about $100 per month.

Postage: $15/month

Once in business, you will be mailing direct mail pieces to your clients, and sending individual brochures and business cards all over the place to get your name out there. Count on at least $15 per month for postage. One way to save a little here is to make your monthly payments for utilities, rent, etc., through online bill payment options.

Rent: $500/month

Rent for the business can run from as little as $300 a month for a small office to $2,000 and upwards for larger spaces depending on the area of the country. Start with an idea of how much space you really need for yourself, your clients, and your equipment. Then check out the places that conform to that size, and ask yourself what adjustments you can make to afford such a space. For example, if you don't have to pay $50 a month for parking, you can add a bit more to your rental costs. Is it okay to move the office further out of town to make your budget work, or will that cut down on your visibility and thus cost you money in the long run?

Be sure to figure the expense of your home mortgage, or your home rental payment, into your overall budget. If that cost is not covered by your spouse's or partner's income, you may want to increase this figure in your budget.

Taxes: $500/month

You'll need to set aside money for quarterly (every three months) tax payments since these funds are not being withdrawn by an employer for social security, or state and federal taxes. If the state you are operating in does not have a state income tax, you can lower this figure. Let's say you have an annual income of $30,000. You should plan to put aside approximately $300 per quarter for the state (only if your state levies a state income tax); and $1,200 per quarter for the federal government (which includes social security and self-employment tax). This is a bitter pill to swallow. It feels like a huge amount of money to a small business person, but failing to plan for, and make, these regular quarterly payments will result in a much greater headache later on. There are penalties for not paying them on time, and if you fail to pay enough tax quarterly, you will end up having to make up the difference all at once on April 15th. Check with your accountant for an accurate figure from the beginning.

Utilities: $50/month

Utilities include whatever you may need to pay for your office utilities. Sometimes, your landlord pays the utlities, and passes the cost on to you through your rent. Check this out with your landlord carefully, especially if you will be using any heating elements on a regular basis in your practice. Also take into account your responsibility for paying your utilities at home—are they covered by a spouse or partner? We're going to list this figure as $50 per month.

Website Retention: $15/month; $30 annually

The company hosting your website will require a monthly payment for the site. This can vary greatly depending on whether or not you are piggy-backing on someone else's site or standing strictly on your own. Charges can range from $5 to over $250 per month depending on how much information your site contains in megabytes (or gigabytes), how often you intend to add additional data to the site, what kind of platform you desire (Linux, Unix, Windows, etc.), and how many email accounts you want to have available for the site (up to 200). We're going to say for the small business owner this is will be about $15 to start, with an additional charge of $30 paid annually for your domain name (the name of your website).

Review of Costs

Initial Set-Up Costs (One-time Only)
Computer: $1,000

Consultant: $1,000 - Cost of an initial consultation with a professional who can explain to you how insurance companies work, and what records you need to keep. Fortunately, you may only need one such meeting.

Equipment: $1,000

Rent: (First and last month of lease, plus security deposit) $1,500

Monthly Budget Categories
Advertising	$50.00
Auto	$550.00
Bank charges	$25.00
Cable	$100.00
Computer and related items	$25.00
Equipment and professional supplies	$150.00
Health insurance	$250.00
Insurance	$125.00
Loan payments	$800.00
Office supplies	$50.00
Parking	$50.00
Personal /Draw	$1,000.00
Phone(s)	$100.00
Postage	$15.00
Rent	$500.00
Taxes	$500.00
Utilities	$50.00
Website Retention	$15.00

Quarterly Costs
Taxes: $1,500 ($300 state and $1,200 Federal)

Annual Costs

Accountant fees: $250

Advertising: brochures and business cards: $200

Auto maintenance: $500

Dues for your professional organization: $200

Domain name fee: $30

Lawyer fees: $250

Licenses and permits: $100

Taxes: any money owed on April 15th after paying quarterly taxes

Remember that your individual expenses may be higher or lower than these figures depending on your practice, your lifestyle, and many other factors. If you have a spouse or partner who covers any of the costs listed above, remove those costs from your budget.

Now the question is how much can you actually make? We will go more thoroughly into setting your fee in another chapter, but for now let's just play with some numbers. Given the figures above, if you charged $70 per hour for each client and you saw 25 clients a week, you would be bringing in $1,750 per week. If you worked 50 weeks a year, that would be $87,500 annually, before taxes.

If you saw ten clients a week, that figure changes to $36,400 per year. You can see how dramatically the figures begin to differ. Realistically, you will see fewer clients in the beginning. A good goal to reach for would be 15 clients a week. This would give you $54,600— enough to cover the costs of the figures above, allowing for $1,000 per month for personal items. Unless you have your own financial backing through family or savings, your business loan will be needed to help you get set up with the proper equipment and supplies. Include in your estimated loan amount enough money to carry you through those first few months, and provide some income while you are out promoting your business.

If these figures seem daunting, remember that your alternative health services are more in demand than ever before. Think and affirm abundance—it's there for the taking. With patience and planning you *can* make this happen.

In addition to the expenses we've covered here, it's important to reinvest in the business. As time goes on, you may want to purchase additional equipment, extend your product line, update your letterhead and brochures, and so on.

Summary

Your choice of office space and the cost of your rent are big considerations. Before you sign a lease, make sure you have figured out how you can cover your initial costs, and what you will need to make on an annual basis. Carefully tailor each of the budget categories listed in this chapter to your particular practice in order to arrive at accurate numbers. To compute a budget that works for you, consider each of the categories and figure out where you can make adjustments.

CHAPTER FOUR

Décor
and Much More

Now we can get into the fun stuff. I will never forget how excited I was to finally have my very own office. I thoroughly enjoyed the first weeks of fixing it up, putting my name on the door, adding some plants to the entrance—all those things. As I fussed over every detail, I mentally blessed the space and it repaid me in kind for many, many years. It probably didn't hurt that my office was in a church— I inhabited the little room in which the former minister had written his sermons. The spiritual setting could not have been better suited to the nature of my work: promoting the holistic health of body, mind and spirit.

I had just enough space for two large counters, one of which I used as a desk with filing cabinets underneath; two comfortable chairs; two bookcases, and a professional light table. When I first moved in, the printing industry was still using paper flats on which I would paste down the contents of the magazine. During my last year of production, 16 years later, I virtually never touched paper since everything was done electronically.

Eventually, I gave up my office and did all of the work from my home so I've had experience with both settings. I was fortunate that I could do that, and I understand that for many of you this is not an option. Some practitioners, for example, would need large spaces in their homes to accommodate their equipment.

For those of you who do decide to rent office space, I want to emphasize the enormous importance of the appearance of the office and its efficient functionality. In my opinion, far too little time is spent on creating a warm, safe, aesthetically pleasing environment for clients, and I don't think it is too extreme to say an office space can make or break a practice. We will address these issues later in the chapter.

Choosing an Office Versus Working at Home

There are pros and cons to working out of your home. On the plus side, it is less expensive because you are not paying additional rent. You are also only paying one set of utility bills. This option can work well if your house has a separate entrance that goes directly to your office; clients should never have to go through your living room to get to your bodywork table. To make such an arrangement work, you need to be an immaculate housekeeper with no dishes in the sink, no laundry on the floor, and no loud music coming from a teenager's bedroom.

Parking is also is a primary concern, especially if your clients may be ill or infirm. Ideally, your driveway should be short, level, and free of snow, children's toys—anything that could inconvenience your clients. One of the disadvantages of working out of your house is that you alone are responsible for whatever the client encounters as an impediment. Is there mold in the basement? Uncut grass? Cluttered newspapers on the front porch? If you have a rental space, all of these cleanup duties are usually the responsibility of the landlord, which gives you a little more free time and less worry, provided the landlord is actually taking care of business.

Many practitioners who start out in their homes to save money eventually move into an office where the space is more private, more professional, and more indicative of a career than a hobby. But, like me, some go in the other direction. You need to consider which environment is best for your business. Too many practitioners get interrupted by their families and friends at home and have trouble setting boundaries between the two. If you do need to start at home, you need to be very clear with your family (and clients) as to what kind of environment you need—and will allow. Are you going to take drop-ins, for example? Whatever you do, do not allow interruptions to your sessions for anything short of a dire emergency. You also want to check with your insurance agent to make sure that your homeowners insurance covers the personal injury of business clients on your property.

The Office Option: Parking

When choosing an office, start by putting yourself in the shoes of your clients. Pretend you have never been to a psychotherapist before, or to a homeopath, or to a skin-roller. You have no idea what to expect, but probably your closest frame of reference is a traditional doctor's office—clean, sterile, and decorated, perhaps, to impersonal perfection.

Now think about what you would *like* to see. The first thing you encounter is the parking lot, or lack thereof. Is there parking on the street? If so, is it free or does it require filling a meter? If there is a meter, does it offer more than one hour of time? Almost no matter what your practice, it will take your clients more than an hour to come and go from your office. If you have an option here, avoid the metered parking.

It may seem silly to dwell on parking but surprisingly it can eventually become one of the things that drives your clients elsewhere, especially if you live in an inclement climate. Without a parking lot or at least parking spaces of your own (that is, your car and your client's car), you run the risk of other parking spaces in town filling up at busy times of the year like holidays, or during special events. You may live in an area that does not give you a great deal of choice, but consider the parking carefully.

Renting and Leasing

Once you have identified the right office space, your next decision will have to do with leases. Some landlords will allow you to rent month to month. This is advantageous to them because it allows them to terminate your tenancy in a very short period of time if they decide you are undesirable. The laws vary from state to state as to how much notice they must give you, and how long you can legally remain. In Massachusetts, a landlord alone cannot evict a tenant; only a judge can order an eviction.

It is more advantageous for you as a practitioner to sign a lease for one-year—the more common arrangement requested by landlords. If the worst-case scenario occurs and you cannot pay the rent for that whole year, you can usually sublet the space, but be sure to check this out in advance. The landlord will most likely agree to this arrangement since it guarantees that he or she will receive the full rent amount. It is within the legal rights of a landlord to request payment for the first month's rent, the last month's rent, a security deposit up to the amount of one month's rent, and the cost of buying and installing a new lock.

Leases are malleable; you can negotiate any given aspect of a lease with the landlord. Although not complicated, leases can contain many clauses with which you are unfamiliar such as the various types of tenancy, the landlord's rights, unfair or deceptive acts on the part of either the landlord or the tenant, repairs, etc. You can familiarize yourself with the laws of the state in which you intend to work or practice by looking up tenant's rights for that state on the Internet; going to your local library; or by writing to the state's Chamber of Commerce. For example, if you go to www.vermont.gov you will find the question: "How Do I Start a Business in Vermont?" When you click on this link it leads you to a page that explains permits and regulations. The permits and regulations page lists a variety of agencies relevant to your situation, and so on. States are most commonly listed on the Internet as either "www.vermont.gov," or with an abbreviation of the state as in "www.state.vt.us" for Vermont, or "www.az.gov" for Arizona. You simply substitute for whichever state you want.

Once you've received a copy of your lease, read it carefully. Do not sign a lease until you are sure you understand exactly what you are signing. Are you able to get out of your lease for a small fee? If not, can you sublet to someone else? Here is where your lawyer comes in handy. Be sure to obtain a copy of your lease agreement in writing.

Do Come In!

Now let's assume you've found your ideal office. Imagine for a moment how it looks to your client. The client just parked her car and is now walking up to the building where you work. What kind of a building is it? Is it a commercial space with several stories? Is it a small apartment building? Is it a slick, contemporary building, or is it a cozy little house serving other professionals? Any one of these can be just fine for your practice as long as it is clear how to find you. What is the path up to your office like? Is there anything in the way of the door, like branches extending too far into the path, or weeds growing up through the cracks in the cement?

What happens once the door is opened? Often the outside door leads to a hall full of other doors. There may be chairs on which the client is expected to sit and wait, or not. There may be a sign on the door that says, "Please knock," or not.

This is where attention to detail can make a big difference. Practitioners should always make clear to their clients, both on the phone when the initial appointment is made, and at the door of the office, how that client should proceed. For example, let's say a client is going to see a bodyworker for the first time for a 2:00 p.m. appointment. She arrives right on time and finds the practitioner's door at the end of the hall. No one is there to greet her—no receptionist, no bodyworker. What should she do? Most likely at around 2:05 p.m., if no one has come out to greet her, she is going to knock on the door, right? But what if the bodyworker is running late and is still in session? The client will have unknowingly disturbed the session, and the bodyworker will have to excuse himself or herself from the client in the session in order to go out and speak to her.

This should never happen. As a practitioner, the worst thing you can do to a first-time customer is cause him or her to feel foolish because of *your* lack of forethought. If there are any complicating factors regarding the entrance to your office or to your procedures, these should all be made very clear on the phone. For example, do your clients know where to sit? Is there reading material for them? Is there a bathroom available or will they need a key to use it? Have you told them you will come out to get them, or should they knock on the door? Be sure to have a sign for your door that indicates whether or not you are in session. Or, if you are out or running late, have a sign that says you will return in five or ten minutes.

I had an experience recently that underscores the importance of making directions to your clients very clear. A massage therapist, whom I was seeing for the first time, and an acupuncturist were sharing an office suite. There was no sign of any kind on the two doors in the darkened hallway that clearly belonged to them, except for their two business cards tacked to only one of the doors. Five minutes after my appointment was to have begun, I knocked on the first door where the cards appeared, but there was no answer. I knocked on the other door and, sure enough, the therapist was in session and asked me to take a seat in the waiting room. What waiting room? I went back to the first door (a solid door with no window) and opened it, half expecting to interrupt a spinal adjustment. Instead I discovered *this* was the waiting room—a very lovely one, too. But who knew?

Unfortunately, even though you give these instructions on the phone, sometimes people forget them by the time they arrive for the appointment because they are too busy wondering if acupuncture hurts, or if chiropractic was the best choice after all. So, as a practitioner, you must inform your clients of these details. If you could possibly be in another session when they arrive, have a sign on your door that says PLEASE DO NOT KNOCK. I WILL BE WITH YOU SHORTLY. Or, if you need to run out suddenly to get some supplies, leave a note on your door specifically addressed to your next client (using their name) explaining that you will be right back. You want to make people feel that whatever process you employ is all part of a plan, that you are a professional and you know what you're doing.

Remember that people are very conscious of their time and it is important for you to be as punctual as possible. People expect to wait for long periods of time occasionally in a traditional doctor's office, but they do not expect to wait in the same way for psychotherapists, and bodyworkers, and frankly, they shouldn't have to. If your client arrives late, explain to them that you understand their reason for being late, but that unfortunately you cannot offer them the full amount of time that day, and give them the opportunity to reschedule. Why? Because your other clients are scheduling themselves in for that long overdue massage on their lunch hour, or for the Rolfing session late in the afternoon that will still allow them to get home on time. By accommodating the late client, you will have inconvenienced all other clients of the day. It may seem unfair that you do not have the same latitude that more traditional practices have with regard to time, but remember that you are trying to carve out your share of the market. To do so, you must understand that for many people, massage is a luxury, not a necessity. Plug your own modality into that last sentence and see if you think it applies.

The Inner Sanctum

What happens when your clients walk into your office? We're going to do a little exercise here for which you'll need a timer. This exercise is what makes a holistic practice very different from a traditional clinical practice. Most holistic therapies such as massage,

EXERCISE

Set the timer for three minutes. Close your eyes and picture your future office in your mind. If nothing comes up immediately just wait a couple minutes. It may take awhile, but it's important that you find some inner view of your office environment.

Imagine walking around in your office. Try to remember everything you see, feel, hear, and smell. Ding! Time is up. What did you see? If nothing appeared, be patient and try it again. You may want to spend some time developing this inner visual skill because it can come in very handy. Write down everything you remember. Later we will return to what you saw. For the following sections, try to imagine what choices you would make as you read to the end of this chapter. Make notes so you can refer to them later.

Rolfing, feldenkrais and psychotherapy are highly personal forms of therapy and the setting needs to reflect that.

Decorating

Before you begin designing your office, you need to think about why clients are coming to you. Usually they have made appointments for one of three reasons: they are in pain (mentally or physically); they are curious; or they want to be pampered. We will discuss motivation later on, but for now, let's just say that in all three cases, they are hoping to find a pleasant, comfortable, and safe setting.

Office decoration receives way too little attention given the impact it can have on your business as a whole, especially since you only have one chance to make a good first impression. Practitioners often try to save money by picking up furniture at yard sales, slapping a coat of paint on the walls, and putting up some posters. There is nothing wrong with this approach, but if you are not a talented decorator, be sure to enlist the help of a friend or family member who can advise you on how to tie everything together in an aesthetically pleasing way.

Think of it this way; this is a room or possibly a suite of rooms, you want your clients to come back to again and again. Each time they come, they should enjoy the feeling they get walking into the room. They may not even be aware of this feeling on a conscious level, but undoubtedly it is having an impact. Before you do anything to your new room, however, be sure to check with your landlord to find out how much change is permissible.

Before even starting to paint, you may want to smudge the room by waving around a tightly wrapped, dried, lighted stick of sage. This is a Native American custom designed to rid the room of any remaining ill will; sealing off any negative history and allowing a new spirit to pervade the space. It also gives the room a wonderful aroma.

Once you have a tentative plan for the arrangement of your room, you may want to consult a feng shui expert before making any permanent moves. A feng shui person can tell you whether the location your door relative to your furniture will allow opportunities to flow in; whether chi (life force energy) in the room can move around unimpeded; and whether any mirrors or pictures are placed to reflect openness and light without bouncing it right back out the door.

Sights: Start with Wall Color

The fashion and preferences in color come in and out of vogue. Recently the most fashionable colors might have been khaki or periwinkle; years ago it might have been mauve or celadon. You can work with most colors in the spectrum as long as whatever goes with them does so in a gentle and complementary fashion, but steer clear of obviously difficult or off-putting colors in neon shades. Black for walls is also not a good idea. Even though a red, white and black color combination can be very attractive, black walls evoke negative feelings. An unfortunate number of people seeking therapy have been traumatized so you want to aim for colors that are upbeat, not dreary. For the same reason, red walls should be handled very carefully. Although red is the color associated with love, it is also associated with danger and anger. It is entirely possible to create a very warm, cozy office with red walls, but they should be softened with lighter colors like pink for pillows or white for the woodwork.

About White

Many practitioners opt for white as the least offensive, most adaptable color for their walls, but white can also be very cold. If you have an office in an old city building with very high ceilings, a solid white room can feel huge and isolating. An all-white room counteracts the feeling of warmth you want to convey. Even if the thermostat says 70° the environment can look and feel frigid. It may say to the client that you couldn't be bothered to provide them with a more comfortable setting; that you just come in, do your work and that's that. Remember that at least some of your clients will come to be pampered.

If you just love white, or your landlord refuses to let you paint your office another color, bring in color from other furnishings like chairs and pillows. In one of my favorite offices, the practitioner left the walls white, but painted all the old pipes that stuck out from the walls different colors. It gave the room some real zip and made you as the client feel energized. It was the perfect touch for a physical therapy practice.

What is your favorite color? If you like dark colors like navy, burgundy or hunter green, use one of those colors for the walls and paint the woodwork white. Buy a patterned rug like an oriental for the floor that combines the wall colors with the others. It is not necessary to buy a true oriental; there are many less expensive versions, as well as tribal rugs and Native American woven wool rugs. If fuchsia and chartreuse (hard colors to deal with) are your thing, soften them with pillows and chairs in more muted colors within the same color palette. Any reputable paint store can provide you with brochures that demonstrate different palettes, and are usually more than happy to give you free paint chips to try out.

Remember when choosing a color that it will intensify once it's on the walls. It's better to err on the lighter side to start with since it's much easier to paint a darker color over a lighter color than the reverse.

You should also know that colors have meaning and impact. Institutional green, for example, has been replaced with pink in some prisons and mental health facilities because of its immediate calming effect. Warm colors include yellow, red, orange, and pink. Yellow promotes creativity. Buddhist monks wear saffron robes to signify renunciation and humility. Red is the color of love and passion, but also, as I mentioned earlier, danger and anger; and orange is the color of happiness and originality, and supposedly has a positive effect on the digestive system.

Think about how the color you choose will dovetail with the climate. For example, if you don't have air conditioning and are practicing bikram yoga in Arizona in the summer; you may not want to paint your office a warm color like orange because the effect will have your clients melting. But if you like orange, a pale apricot would be a nice compromise.

Blues, greens, and purples constitute cool colors. Blue is the color associated with depth and peace, green with abundance and fertility, and purple with both death and higher consciousness. Whatever meaning you take from a color, there is always a beautiful shade of that hue that is usable.

Wallpaper, of course, is another option for the walls, but it is much more expensive than paint. If you decide on wallpaper, choose something that appears to give a texture to the walls as opposed to patterns with little symmetrical designs or large flowery prints. The walls should not overwhelm the inhabitants. Remember you are trying to create something that is not reminiscent of the often-antiseptic allopath's office, but a comfortable, warm space for individual human beings.

Another consideration for the walls is notices. Unfortunately many people have a tendency to scribble a quick reminder about returning tapes, or not parking in the driveway, or whatever it is, and just tack them up on the wall. These handmade signs always look sloppy. They're not homey and cute; they're just messy looking. If you need some signs for reminders, and can't afford a permanent, professionally made sign, at least go to a stationery store and buy laminating sheets that fit on a 8.5 inch by 11-inch sheet of paper. Use a laser-printed rendition of whatever it is you want to say, laminate it, and hang it in a fashion that connotes care as opposed to indifference.

Furniture and Furnishings

If your practice involves a bodywork table, you will want the table positioned in the center of the room with lots of space on either side. Always make sure that you have a movable and steady two-step platform up to the table for shorter or infirm clients who have trouble moving. How much other furniture is necessary? The answer depends on your particular practice and the size of the room. Ideally, you will have a desk where you can make notes, a chair for the desk, an additional chair for your clients, and a table and/or cabinet for any products you will be using. This is the bare minimum, but it can still be completely functional.

Figure out where you want to put your sound system. Do you need a separate table or can you manage with it on the floor in a corner where it will not be in the way? Make sure you have hangers for coats, or a coat stand that is securely anchored and will not fall down.

Before choosing furniture, think about the overall feeling in the room and of the type of clients you are hoping to attract. The room will tell the client a lot about you with the first glance. Is it a spare, contemporary environment? If so you may want furniture with un-complicated lines and a minimalist feel, but remember to add touches of warmth, like a red pillow. Is it a cozy, romantic space that Victorians would love? If so, you may want an upholstered antique loveseat, but will your male clients feel comfortable in such a space? You just need to consider all the aspects of your clientele.

It is not necessary to spend a lot of money on furnishings, but they must be clean, painted or polished. Whatever you decide you want to create for your clients, there should be cohesiveness to the look and the room should be welcoming to all. If the room looks well put together, it suggests that your practice is well put together. If you spend some time on this and do it right, you will be able to keep it this way for years.

Lighting

Lighting, too, is very important to the look and feel of the room. Overhead lighting is unfortunate, but necessary for some practices. You can soften the feel of the overhead interrogation-lamp effect by using a pink bulb. For other lamps in the room, you can buy natural spectrum bulbs, which are also eco-friendly, in several different watt-ages. The lighting should be strong enough for you to be able to see what you're doing, but not so strong that it renders the room imper-sonal and uncomfortable.

If the overhead light is fluorescent, that's a problem. You may want to ask your landlord to change it to incandescent and if he or she refuses, offer to pay for it yourself. It will probably cost you any-where from $65 to $200 for the installation, plus the cost of the fixture ($100 and up). Fluorescent lighting has nothing to do with the natural or holistic realm, and it makes a buzzing noise that would be very disruptive to clients whether they are there for psychotherapy or a yoga class.

Extras

Go green! Plants and fresh flowers are welcome in any office. If you have a plant, or even a tree, make sure it is well cared for, clipped to a reasonable size, and anchored securely so it can't be knocked over. Avoid flowers that have an overpowering redolence, like lilies, and any large flower arrangements that may sit between you and your client (especially for psychotherapists).

As far as wall décor, posters are fine if nicely framed, but signed prints, oils, and pastels are better if you can afford them. It is not necessary to overwhelm clients with your art collection or even your own attempts at art, but it is a good idea to have a pleasant, tasteful focus on the walls—not posters tacked up with scotch tape.

In addition, you want to underscore your professionalism, no matter what holistic field you are practicing. Even though you know that the term "massage therapy" has outrun it's predecessor—the "massage parlor"—with all its innuendoes, there are still people who are circumspect about actually receiving a massage. For example, anyone who has experienced any kind of physical abuse will need to feel very safe in your office. Therefore, you should make your certification(s) visible on a wall. And, you should spell out any degrees that you've earned. Many people have no idea what LMT (Licensed Massage Therapist) stands for, as obvious as it may seem to you. Everything you can point to that supports your professional expertise will be reassuring to your clients.

Toward that end, if you have not already done so, you should join the regional and national professional organizations, societies, or associations that support your particular field. You do not have to attend every meeting, of course, but you will receive the literature from these organizations, which will keep you up-to-date. Your joining demonstrates a professional interest to your clients. You will want to include any such organization in the brochure that you will have available, both in your office and around town.

About Smells

Second to what people see is what they smell; our olfactory senses are very sensitive. It is said that a certain scent can evoke a memory sooner than a song. It's very helpful and soothing to the client to have some form of aromatherapy or essential oils present in the room, as long as they are not allowed to become too strong. Think mild and pleasant. As a practitioner, you should avoid wearing perfume or a personal scent of any kind since many clients are allergic to the alcohols in perfumes and body washes.

Climate plays a role in a scent sense. If you live in New England, for example, for at least several months of the year you and your clients are sloshing through ice and snow. You come in with wet boots and walk on the carpet. Inevitably your carpet picks up the odor. And where do you leave the boots you have removed? Or those of your client? You don't want either of those odor-producing agents within an offending distance of the client's nose. Either post a sign asking clients to leave their boots outside your door before they enter, or have a box or closet where they can be stored for the session.

We all have a tendency to become acclimated to our own spaces and can lose our sensitivity to what that space might smell like to someone else. You may want to have a small fan going to make sure the room doesn't get too stuffy, and be aware of eating garlic, onions, and other spicy foods at lunch. They are strong smells that stay with the body for hours, so wash your hands and pop in a breath mint before greeting clients with these odors. There is nothing worse than being breathed on by someone with phlegm breath during the cold season so take care to remember your honey drops.

Check the smell of your office regularly and if you have sinus problems and can't smell well, ask a friend to come in and give you an honest opinion. Have the carpeting or the rugs in your office cleaned at least once a year. Steam cleaning is the best way to do this, and you can probably rent a steam-cleaner from your local grocery, hardware or rental store. If for any reason you cannot clean your own office on a weekly basis, or are not inclined to do so, hire a service for this purpose.

Take Another Look

By now the walls are painted, the furniture is in place, the plant is in the corner. Take another look around. Is there unsightly clutter on the desk? Is the wastebasket overflowing? What more could you do to present an appearance of comfortable efficiency? If you have enough space, you might want to ad a partition for clients to change behind even though you are not in the office when they are changing. It just adds an air of privacy. Or you may want to use a screen to hide your desk and papers from view.

What Do You Hear?

Soft music is essential for most holistic bodywork practitioners. There is no right or wrong with regard to musical choice as long as the music is appropriate for the practice. Bluegrass banjo or knee-slapping country tunes are probably not the best choices for massage therapists, for example. There is some lovely new age music available, but some of it can be repetitive and boring. Soft classical music is usually welcome, but opera may be a turn-off to some clients. The first criterion for music is that it must be relaxing. Also, it's important to know the difference between soothing and sad or melancholy.

One of the more destructive things that can happen during a session is that your sound system goes awry. As you know, your work with your hands takes on a certain rhythm once you begin a massage or a Rolfing session. If a CD starts skipping, or if the music stops entirely, the whole session is unnecessarily interrupted. Get a good head cleaner for your system and use it regularly. Sometimes CDs just go bad, so be sure to test them before your sessions.

Also, if your office has thin walls, especially if you are a psychotherapist, you may want to invest in a white noise machine. These are relatively small machines that cost about $50 and can be placed out of the way on the floor. They create a constant din that masks conversations taking place in the room next door. Look for one that has several levels of sound; if you buy one that has only an on and off switch, you may discover the noise is too loud. These machines can heat up, so whatever you do, don't try to muffle the sound by putting a pillow over the machine. Look for another model or a better solution.

How Does It Feel?

The things your clients come in contact with in your office should feel as comfortable as the rest of it. Sheets for bodywork tables, for example, are most likely knits so that thread count is irrelevant, but sheets should be made of 100% cotton if possible. Buy top quality; the sheets will be washed frequently and can become scratchy or full of pills in no time. Some people have very sensitive skin, either by nature, or because of medications they may be taking, so softness is important.

There are some important things to know about sheets. They can be classified as "organic," "green" or "natural." Only "organic" cotton comes from farmers who conform to strict national standards for raising their plants and animals, and operating without herbicides and pesticides. Linens labeled "natural" or "green," however, can be made from products grown with pesticides, but are not treated at the end of the production process with chemicals like formaldehyde, and are not bleached with chlorine. Inspection of goods labeled "natural" or "green" appears to be haphazard, so it may be difficult to tell whether or not they adhere to standards.

Check stores and catalogs for products made out of natural fibers and companies that give a percentage of their profits to the environment. Your clients will appreciate your total health consciousness on their behalf, as well as your concern for the global village. Remember, you want to walk your talk.

Does It Sparkle?

Now it's time to take a look around again. The wall color looks terrific with the new furniture—or the furniture you got at a yard sale and painted. The rug brings it all together, but how *clean* is it? Here is where we *do* want to emulate the antiseptic allopath's office. Your office should be spotless. Any flat surfaces in the room such as your desk should reflect the light; the floor should be vacuumed; the lamps and lamp shades should be dusted; every implement should be cleaned or sterilized; the walls should be clear of spots; the corners free of dust balls and cobwebs; and the linens free of any sign of dirt or wear. Naturally, any bathrooms used by your clients should also be clean and checked regularly after each client's use. I know you don't do this at home, but this is your business we're talking about. You cannot possibly go wrong with an immaculate space, but you can drive clients right out the door with even a hint of someone else's body oils, dirt, dust, or mold; or a toilet that hasn't been cleaned.

I once took my daughter to an acupuncturist who had a very good reputation. The waiting area was furnished with upholstered chairs from a rummage sale whose cushions sagged badly. There were spots and stains resulting from many elbows resting on the arms, and as I looked across at the walls, I noticed grimy, black stains swirling up the paint from too many winters next to the radiator. I was about to tell my daughter we were leaving, when the acupuncturist opened her door to a very lovely, well-kept office.

As it turned out this practitioner was worth her weight in gold, and greatly helped my daughter's condition, but we almost didn't stay long enough to find this out. All it would have taken was a new coat of paint and a clean chair to render her waiting area up to standards. Was she responsible for the waiting area or was her landlord? It didn't matter. She almost lost some clients because it looked so tawdry. In cases like this it's worth your while to work with your landlord for improvements.

One More Time

Now that you're satisfied you've covered all the bases, imagine going through your new office as a person with some stiffness, or someone who is undergoing chemotherapy, or recovering from recent surgery. Is there a place to sit down and rest? Will they feel welcome in your office? Can they reach the table comfortably?

Let's return to your original vision of your office with our three-minute exercise and compare it to your choices after considering the suggestions made above. How close are they? If they are very close, you won't have much trouble getting started. If they are farther apart, this is important information for you. It suggests that you need to pay close attention to these little details because they do not come as naturally to you as they might to someone else. This does not need to hold you back—you just may need a little more help creating your ideal office space. We are all wired differently; some of us are more intuitive, others more logical, but we can all successfully pursue our career goals as long as we know what tools to use along the way. Think of your office as a place where magic happens; clients enter in a certain condition, and are totally transformed by the time they leave. What does magic *look like* to you?

Summary:

The appearance and the setting of your office can have a huge impact on your clients, and therefore on your business. It is worth your time and effort to make sure you've taken care of every detail. Then you can relax and forget about it since this is not something you will have to do every day. Just think about who your clients are, and how you can make them feel welcome in your new space.

CHAPTER FIVE

All Systems Go!

Now that you've arranged the office, you can begin to think about what supplies you will need, and what office systems you want to employ for bookkeeping, scheduling appointments, storing client information and so on. In an earlier age, much of this work would have been accomplished through handwritten ledgers, tally sheets, and file folders stored in desk drawers. Today computers make all these tasks much easier to complete. Unfortunately, some people in our holistic realm are phobic about computers. If this applies to you, relax. Computers are going to make your working life a piece of cake, at least as far as all the paperwork aspects of it goes.

It can be very frustrating trying to keep up with all the latest technological devices, especially for the non-technically-inclined, but the truth is, in order to be business-savvy, you must be computer savvy—at least to a certain extent. You don't, however, have to know every aspect of every piece of software. For example, there are many commands and facets of Microsoft Word that many people never use at all. So, what do you need for a workable business system?

Types of Computers

First you must have a computer. In order to succeed in business—any kind of business—you must be able to speak the language of your bank, your clients, and your vendors—all of whom are most likely using computers for business, pleasure, or both. Besides, computers offer the most efficient and versatile way of tracking your clients, keeping your books, recording payments, and scheduling appointments.

When I started out in business, I was using a Mac SE, a small, but heavy computer that was also incredibly slow. Today it is considered a dinosaur. Now, there are many different varieties of personal computers that are used for word processing, navigating the Internet, sending emails and faxes, watching DVDs and listening to music. For the small business owner, software that stores data such as the names and addresses of your clients, will be critical. Often such software comes pre-installed on a newly purchased computer. We will go over the options available and the varieties of computers that exist, but pricing will not appear in these pages due to the rapidly changing markets for such things. Generally speaking, however, it has been the case over the last decade that Macs (Apple Macintosh) are more expensive than PC's (Dell, IBM, etc.) when comparing comparable functions and assets.

Personal computers can come in the form of desktops, laptops, PDA's (personal digital assistants such as Blackberrys and Treos), tablet computers and wearable computers. Desktop computers are designed for use at the home or office and can appear as home or personal computers, servers or workstations. Workstations are used for manipulating complex data relevant to engineering and mathematics, and servers provide services to other computing systems. If you foresee a need to move your computer frequently, you may want a laptop (also known as a notebook), which is a single component that weighs very little and is easily transported in a carrying case. If you need to take work home, or use your computer outside the office, the laptop is the best bet. You can add attachments that will give you access to a printer, a wireless router, an external document/data saver to backup your files, and a modem. Each of these devices can be easily detached for movement from one place to another, and all of these attachments or functions can also be part of a desktop computing system.

PDA's originated as hand-held devices that could contain an address book, a calendar, a notepad, word processing software, and could also allow game playing. They have evolved to include much broader functions and can now access the Internet; serve as a phone, video or audio unit for watching movies or listening to music; can access wireless networks; and even employ GPS (global positioning system) navigation. Physicians can now use them to access pharmaceutical information for their patients instantaneously.

Some PDA's have touch screens that are activated with a stylus (a pencil-like tool). Others have thumb wheels and a full keyboard. All are a size that can fit into your pocket. The advantage to these small devices is that they can go everywhere you go. The disadvantage is that because they are so small and mobile, they are also very easy to lose. If all your data is stored in only this one place, you could easily lose it all. Fortunately, most PDA's have the capacity to be synchronized with PC's, but this requires purchasing both the handheld device and a desktop or laptop computer.

A tablet computer is shaped like a chalk slate and is smaller than a laptop, but larger than a PDA. They are operated by a fingertip or a stylus instead of a keyboard or mouse. Wearable computers are literally worn on the body, look like wristwatches, and allow for total hands-free operation while recording information. These computers have very limited applications, mostly for doctors, and are irrelevant for business purposes.

In my opinion, all of your needs can easily be met by a laptop computer. I've used a Mac for years because of the intuitive design, but I'm sure any PC laptop would accommodate your needs. Today there are software programs that can be used on both Macs and PCs, which was not always the case.

What Kinds of Software Do You Need?

You will need a good word processing program like Microsoft Office which is available for both Macs and PC's, and includes a number of subprograms like Microsoft Word, Excel, Power Point and Outlook Express. In addition to allowing you to write letters, programs like this can also be used to create your own advertisements since they will import graphics. You will also need a good database management system for keeping client files and recording notes about your clients, as well as financial recordkeeping software. At some point, you might want a program designed to calculate your taxes, but for now, word processing, database management, and financial recordkeeping are the most important types of software you'll need.

Using Word Processing Software

You can use your word processing software to produce copies for printing brochures, name cards, press releases, and all other materials you might need for promotional purposes. We will address this in more detail in a later chapter, but it is important to remember because you can save a lot of money producing your own materials instead of paying a graphic artist to produce them for you. As with all your software, spend some time becoming familiar with the various commands. Once you figure out how to insert a graphic to your brochure text, or how to merge letters so that you can personalize them with your clients' names, make your own notes for quick reminders on how to perform these tasks. Doing so will save you time in the long run. When you don't use commands frequently, it's easy to forget what they are. Manuals can be helpful, but your own words are better.

Using Database Management Software

Database management software (DBMS) allows you to keep a record for each of your clients and make notes about them. By creating categories for retrieving that information, you can create reports for various aspects of your business. Say, for example, you want to know how many of your clients are coming to you with a frozen shoulder. If you have established categories for particular injuries, you can simply enter the information and voila! You should be able to tailor your software to accommodate all the categories you need to retrieve.

Your software should allow spaces for all of the obvious bits of information like name, address, phone number, cell phone number, and email address, but it should also provide you with a space for making notes about your clients. These notes are intended for your eyes only, but they can be enormously useful for other reasons if taken on a regular basis. They can include personal bits of information that may be useful to you in terms of understanding your clients. Jim's daughter was still recovering from a car accident when he came in last November. No wonder he was so tense! "Is your daughter better now?" you can ask at his next visit because you will have checked your notes before he arrives. It can be very difficult when you see many people in a week to remember each client's personal story, but there is nothing worse for a client than going to a session only to find that the person he poured his heart out to at the last sesson, has no memory of his personal trauma. In the practice of holistic health, this is very bad form, so make sure you have a way of taking quick notes after each session.

Database management software also enables you to design your own forms for obtaining information from your clients. For example, when you see a client for the first time, you will want to have him or her fill out a form with all relevant medical information as in Appendix B. You can set this up on your computer so that forms can be printed easily and are ready for you whenever you need them. If you print ten at a time, you will have extras on hand in case your computer is down.

There are several different possibilities for database management software, but one thing to consider is what the program will look like on the screen. For example, Microsoft Excel is a spread sheet that runs across the page, while FilemakerPro allows for a single record to be configured in whatever way the user chooses. Another feature to consider is the program's flexibility. Will you be able to manipulate the data in a variety of ways? Does it allow you to create a list of all the people who came to your office last spring, or would it be able to list all your clients from the ages of 25 to 35? MySQL (or PostgreSQL) is another program worth investigating because it's free, and users claim that it has greater flexibility than other database management systems. You may not even be able at this point to project how you might want to use a database program in the future, so try to choose one that allows for the greatest flexibility. Experiment with the programs available in order to decide which will be easiest to use before making a purchase since keeping records will become a very important part of your business day.

A Note About RecordKeeping

Record-keeping is an essential feature of any business, but it is particularly important for the sole proprietor since you have no other employees to whom you can turn if your memory fails. Many, if not most, states require a written record of each interaction with a client which should include a treatment plan, target goals, notes about problems that arise, questions from the client, and other details. Such notes may be a saving grace if you are ever sued by a client. You may not be guilty of any wrongdoing, but if you have no log with which to make your defense, it will be that much easier to make a case against you.

If the law in your state requires written records and you are not keeping them, or are only keeping them sporadically, you may find yourself without an occupation if you get caught. Sometimes, if written records are not required, you might be able to tape record notes. Check the laws in your state. If yours is a state that has no requirements, or the requirements are minimal, understand that if you fail to keep track of client interactions in a way that can be easily presented to a court, you may suffer the consequences.

How long are you required to keep records and what is the correct way to dispose of them? You'll want to keep any business-related records for seven years. This includes leases, contracts, insurance forms, tax returns, cancelled checks, sales records, and any ledgers or journals in which you've made notations about profits and losses. If you are strictly using your computer to make these notations, make sure you print out this information on a regular basis so that you have hard copies. Thoroughly shred any paperwork when it is time to discard it.

Shareware, Freeware, and Open Source Software

There have been some interesting developments in the software industry since the establishment of proprietary software companies that have huge implications for small business owners trying to save money. These companies have dominated the software market. In addition to paying the high cost of their software ($300 to $1,000 per program), users are obliged to sign a license that prevents them from distributing or sharing in any way, the information stored on the application disc that comes with the program. Theoretically, this means that in some cases, business owners would be obliged to purchase a separate program license for each of their employees to use. Also, because of the way the software is written, it isn't possible for users to see the source code or understand how the software works, let alone tweak it for any adjustments that might be needed to suit a particular business. Moreover, users are completely dependent on the company for assistance if anything should go wrong with the software.

Over time, other similar options such as shareware and freeware appeared. Shareware is software available through the Internet. Users can download the application, try it out for a certain period of time (usually 30 days), and then decide if they want to actually buy it. At the end of the stipulated time period, if no action has been taken to purchase the software, the shareware will either stop working altogether, or certain features of the program will be locked until a registration code (from a purchase) is evident.

Freeware is free in one way, but not in another. It's free in the sense that the user can download it and use it without any cost or restriction. It is not free in the sense that the source code is not available, the software cannot be distributed freely, and it is not possible to make any changes to the program itself.

Yet another permutation of the software industry occurred in the 1980s when Richard M. Stallman launched the "free software" movement, the culmination of which is a GNU/Linux-based operating system. As a programmer at MIT, Stallman grew impatient and frustrated by the restricted use of the Unix mainframe and decided to write his own software, which he licensed under the principle of "copyleft" as oppposed to copyright. His notion of educaton, which by its very nature involves sharing information freely, didn't mesh with the operational nickel-and-diming that was taking place across the country with regard to computer software.

Open-source software allows users to view the source code of the program, make changes to it, and share the information with other users who employ the GNU Public Licenses (GPL), Stallman's trademark software license. The open source software that corresponds to Microsoft Office is called OpenOffice.org, and the open source knock-off of Photoshop is called Gimp (Gnu Image Manipulation Program). In adddition to MySQL, these programs are a much less expensive alternative to proprietary software, possibly saving a new business owner hundreds of dollars in start-up money. The down-side is that there is no company to turn to if problems arise, but advocates claim there are many other users available to chat with online for the purpose of problem solving.

Additional Software

So far, we've been talking about software that allows you to keep track of your clients, and software you can use for letters, brochures, and promotional materials. Another category of software has to do with keeping track of your finances. If you have never kept books before for the purpose of business, you are in for a treat. Software programs like Quicken and Quick Books (the opensource equiva-lent is GnuCash), make the notation of income and expenses so easy that even the least experienced practitioner can do it. Quicken is traditionally used for addressing your personal financial accounts and Quick Books is geared toward business accounting. Through Quicken Books you will enter each expense as it occurs, and each payment from a client as you collect it. At the end of the month, you will get a bank statement that you can easily reconcile through this program, and know exactly where you are financially at all times.

If you are not a detail-oriented person, or not inclined to keep tabs daily on your accounts, I highly recommend that you set up online banking with your local bank. Before I had Quicken I used what's called a One-Write, a ledger in which I made all of my financial notations by hand. Adding up the columns took forever and I would often get different figures when I double-checked them. I would forget bank fees and automatic drafts. Online banking changed all that for the better. Now, every time I get a statement, I balance the online checkbook that day. I can't tell you how happy that Quicken program makes me when it says "Congratuations! You're all Balanced!"

Another function of bookkeeping programs is to present you with reports on your income. You can request a standard report or you can customize the report to suit your needs. These reports will show you how much you spend in a week, a month or a year on each one of your budget line items. Without fumbling around trying to analyze cost/benefit ratios, you can simply press a button and your answers will appear. All you have to do is record entries on a regular basis.

These programs will also save you money with your accountant. If an accountant has to go over your handwritten books, it will take more time, and therefore cost you a lot more money, than if you simply provide him or her with a report from your studiously kept financial notes on your computer. With your notes, your accountant can estimate your quarterly taxes. He or she should provide you with the exact amout of your state income tax, and your federal income tax with envelopes and forms to be mailed every three months to the two government offices. Accountants will charge an additional amount to finalize your yearly taxes in April, but it will cost you much less if you have been using your software properly.

I also recommend that you pay bills online. Anything that will streamline your day is worth it. This process is quick, easy, and costs you nothing—no stamps, no envelopes. This is also one thing we can all do to green up the planet since it reduces the amount of paper transactions required.

Spend some time with the software when you first have it installed so that you can play around with the various functions before you actually open your office. It's very important that you know exactly how you are going to record information of all types so that you can do it quickly and easily on a regular basis.

Furthermore, remember to back up the information every day to a source that is outside of your computer. If you are using a laptop, you can insert a very tiny little gizmo called a thumb drive (also called a jump drive) that will allow you to store all your information such as client files. This detaches from your computer so that if your computer is ever totally damaged for some reason, you will not have lost all your information.

I should add that there is also tax software, like eFile, that enables you to do your own taxes. Although this may come in handy down the road, I would strongly advise you to work with your accountant for the first few years until you have a really good feel for how to identify deductions, and until you're familiar with the tax forms you'll need to file. Otherwise, you risk spending more money by missing certain business deductions, or worse, you don't pay the full amount of taxes to the IRS.

Staying on Top of it All

One of the biggest drags in any business is the paperwork. I don't know many people who really enjoy dealing with requisite papers, forms, bills and notices. As a consequence, many of us are inclined to look at the pile of paper and say "Not today!" Unfortunately it doesn't take long for the pile to grow, and before you know it, it's blocking the light from the window. Do not let this happen. You can reduce the amount of time you spend on paperwork to minutes a day, versus hours and hours on weekends, if you follow some pretty simple rules.

First, before your first client arrives on Monday morning, you are going to look up her file and refresh your memory about her condition, particularlities, etc., by reading your computer notes. Immediately after your session with her, you are going to make additional notes. You will do this for each client throughout the day.

At the end of the day, you will go through your mail, immediately enter any bills and any payments for that day into Quicken. And then you back it up and that's it! Done. Or, you may decide to perform these tasks first thing in the morning, logging information from the previous day. The important concept here is *daily*. If you do these very small things on a daily basis, managing your business will not become onerous.

Help When You Need It

We've already talked about the importance of cultivating relationships with your lawyer and your accountant. Another extremely useful relationship is the one you will inevitably have with your computer technician. If you are a do-it-yourselfer, you may be able to figure out your computer problems, but if not, your computer techie can prove vital to your business.

Computers never crash or breakdown at convenient times, because there is no such thing. Judith Orloff, a best-selling psychotherapist, coined the term "techno-despair" for the special kind of misery resulting from computer failures, including the loss of pages and pages of documents due to a failure to back them up. Ever done that? Fortunately it's awful enough so that it trains you to back up your information all the time. Yes, computer problems foster a kind of panic and despair that was unknown before their invention.

If your computer goes on the blink, and you can't fix it yourself, you'll have to call a techie, and wait until the computer is fixed to resume your entries, making handwritten notes in the meantime. You want this time to be shorter rather than longer, so don't wait until your computer goes berserk. Go out before you open your practice and talk to some of the technicians in your town. Explain what your situation will be and ask them what their availability is on short notice. Remember that they are in business, too. If they can see that you might be a regular customer if you can work out an arrangement, they are likely to be interested.

I used to have someone come to my office to fix my computer because it was large and hooked up to what seemed like a million accessories. The wires alone were completely daunting and all of it was stuffed into a very tight space. If I had a problem, I had no idea where to start, and of course, computer disasters *always* happened right at deadline time. I had a wonderful group of folks at that time who came and rescued me, and naturally, I purchased all my software from them. Years later, I had an arrangement with them that enabled me to talk to them on the phone when I needed to fix a problem. Over time, I've learned how to fix many of these things myself. I'm not encouraging that at this point, but I will say that if I can do it, so can you.

Office Supplies You Will Need

What do you need to have immediately at your fingertips? Let's start with your desk. Obviously you want your business cards and brochures out in plain sight. You will need pens, paper for any quick notes, Kleenex for you or your clients, medical forms that you've designed, appointment reminder cards for your clients, envelopes, and any educational literature about your craft. These latter pieces can be very helpful for patients who have questions about your work. They can reinforce your own explanations of what you will be doing, what the client can expect from a session, and what the result is likely to be. If you have a suite of offices, have shelves installed that will hold all your policy sheets, medical intake forms, and literature in each room where you expect to see clients. You don't want to have to leave the room every time you need a form.

You will also want your one-and-only appointment book available. Using more than one book to record your appointments can be a hazard; it makes mistakes almost inevitable. Keep it in a predictable spot on your desk. Also, be sure to take it home at night in case you wake up feeling sick the next day, so you can easily contact your clients to cancel their appointments.

The main thing to remember about your desk is that is says quite a bit about you and your practice. You may be an extraordinarily good nutritionist, working wonders with your patients, but if your desk is a mess, it connotes a lack of organization on your part. In turn, this suggests a slap-dash approach to your business. This may seem like a ludicrous conclusion to you, but there is no sense fighting it; it is a fact. What you *want* to convey to your clients is that you care so much about your business, that you have taken the time to think of every detail. Do they have questions about "x?" Here is the brochure to answer those questions. If a client asks what your policies are regarding payment and cancellation, you can immediately reach for your printed policy sheet explaining all of those things.

Your desk needs to reflect order and efficiency. If you normally thrive in the middle of clutter and can't find the surface of your desk, now is the time to try learning a new habit. Believe me, it will make everything so much easier. Setting up your desk so that you can easily grab whatever you need in a hurry, without having to scrounge around in a pile of papers, will have a big impact on your clients as well. Make sure you know exactly where you put what. If you have file drawers, make the labels large enough and readable enough so that you can locate any given file quickly.

One of the things you can do to help differentiate yourself from other practitioners is pay attention to the personal details of people's lives. Pre-paid postcards (at 28¢ each 100 costs $28) and a tickler file can help you do this in an organized way. Inevitably you will talk to clients and they will confide in you. In some cases you might learn more than you ever wanted to know. If a client comes in because they are anxious about surgery that is scheduled two weeks from now, take notice. As soon as the client leaves, write a little note wishing them good luck with the surgery and place it in your tickler file to be mailed just before they have the surgery done. Tickler files can be purchased at most stationery stores, and are organized by month with 30 to 31-day slots for each month. People never forget this kind of thoughtfulness.

Also, if you find out about the death of a friend or relative of one of your clients, don't hesitate to send flowers or make a donation to their favorite charity. Such gifts are always a demonstration of caring, and its one occasion when you shouldn't even think about the cost. Just do it. Even if you're stone-broke, the good karma will come back to you—and again, this kind of response to a tragedy is never forgotten.

Other things you may want to mark are birthdays, business anniversaries, and special holidays. If you find an article in the newspaper about one of your clients, clip it out and send it to your client in case he or she might want an extra copy. When I found such an article, I used to attach a simple post-it note and fired it off that day. Another cardinal rule: put it in writing. If someone has sent you a gift or done something nice for you, a hand-written, pre-paid postcard is so handy for saying thank you. Email is very impersonal for this purpose. These little things are generally a good rule in life, but for a personal business such as yours, they will be essential.

Professional Supplies

Order, cleanliness, and efficiency are a must here as well. Your clients will find it difficult to believe that those acupuncture needles are clean (even if you're taking them out of their wrappers right before their eyes), if your office is a mess—or worse—dirty. Remember that even though you are very familiar with your craft and that acupuncture, just as one example, has become almost commonplace in some regions, there are also those patients who are coming to you because nothing else has worked and they are desperate, skeptical, and scared. Every move you make from wrapping them in a nice, warm blanket, to lighting the moxibustion, should put them at ease.

Each practice has its own paraphernalia. As much as possible, your equipment or products, like aromatherapy oils, should be stored neatly in a bookcase on the wall. Check the shelf life of any products you sell carefully and discard anything that has outlived its expiration date. Anything that is visible should be kept out of the path of clients, children, and anyone else who may have accompanied the client. My chiropractor always has a corner full of children's toys so that they can be entertained while the parent is getting spinal adjustments. This may be inappropriate for your particular practice, but when possible, including room for children is a plus. Perhaps they can play with the physioballs while Mom is on the Pilates machine.

Now that we've taken care of the aesthetics, dealt with the office and professional supplies, as well as computers and software, we're ready to start bringing in the clients.

Summary

A laptop computer will probably be able to address all your computing needs. Choose your business software carefully, experimenting with several different types, and pick the ones that both appeal to you on the screen and cover all your requirements. You will need word processing software, database management software, and bookkeeping software.

Establish a relationship with a technical person who can help you in times of computer crisis. Don't wait until you're desperate. Try to establish a process by which you can get help from this person on an emergency basis such as by email or phone.

Think about the supplies you will need for your business in general, and for your practice in particular. Make sure your supplies can be easily retrieved, and are neatly arranged on your desk and in bookcases or other furnishings.

CHAPTER SIX

Show Me
the Money!

Setting Your Fee

With your strong legal and business systems foundation, to which you've added an aesthetically pleasing office space, you're almost ready to start meeting your clients. Before this can happen, you need to identify the fees you will be charging for your services. Naturally, you will want to charge as much as the market will bear. One way to identify this figure, is to find out what other therapists in your area are charging. Go to the Yellow Pages, find other therapists in your field, and call to ask them what they charge. Check with your local Chamber of Commerce to see if there are particular therapists who are recommended, and contact those therapists. Search the Internet, and read through the ads in your local newspaper or holistic health magazine. You can also check with your national association or organization for regional information regarding fees and charges.

As a newcomer you may have to start at the bottom, but don't be discouraged about this. As your business grows, you can begin to raise your fees. If your area has a large number of massage therapists who do exactly what you do, and you are brand new to the game, you may have to lower your initial fee in order to get a slice of the market. For example, if the going rate is $50 an hour, you may need to start at $45. In the beginning, you must factor into the equation your lack of experience. This can actually be a plus because it means that you can set your fees slightly lower than other therapists in your area. People always love a bargain. You don't want to set fees too low, however, because too low a fee suggests desperation, a gross lack of expertise, or both. On the other hand, if you are the only person in your area who does deep tissue massage, you might be able to charge the $50 an hour fee.

Initially, you will want to concentrate your efforts on getting more clients who pay less money. As you get better at what you do, and begin to distinguish yourself from other therapists, you can start accepting fewer clients and charging more money. This amounts to more hard work for you at first, but it leads down the road to fewer clients, or at least a comfortable number of them, who are willing to pay a higher fee for the wonderful skills you've developed.

Think about whether your practice is one that lends itself to an hourly rate, or a rate per session, and what your session length is likely to be. Do you have extras you can charge for such as hot towels, herbal teas, or the use of a hot tub after a massage? A chiropractor I know charges a relatively low fee of $36 per session. His secretary schedules 15-minute sessions throughout the day, and it is not unusual for him to see 18 clients in a single day. The low rate is attractive, his services are vital, and yet if he needs to take more than the 15-minutes allotted, he will. Sometimes this means his clients have to wait, but it doesn't seem like a terrible inconvenience since his rate is so low. His low rate also encourages the use of his services on a regular basis, making it possible for lower income people to afford him. He probably grosses well over $100,000 annually.

Let's go back to Chapter Three and look at your budget. If you've determined that other therapists in the area are charging between $50 and $100 an hour for their services, what would be a reasonable fee for you to charge? Let's say you decide you can manage with 30 clients a week who pay only $45 an hour, but you don't want to stand out as the person on the bottom of the totem pole. You can turn this lower rate into a plus by advertising it as a special "new office" offering. Once you have enough regular clients, you can begin to play with other pricing formulas.

An ingenious friend of mine, a massage therapist, began by offering the first session for free. Yes, no strings attached. She was confident enough in her ability to believe that once her clients experienced her deft little fingers on their backs, they would return—and she was right. Offering freebies is always a winner, as long as you can truly afford it. If you factor into your business loan request the money you'll need for your first few months, you may be able to afford such offerings. Her clients then paid the full hourly rate when they returned for their second session.

As time went on and the market changed, she needed to adopt new strategies for keeping her business afloat financially. She advertised the first half hour as free and requested payment for the second half hour. This did not mean that she literally cut her hourly rate in half. Instead she actually raised her hourly rate enough to suit her budget, but at the same time offered her clients a bit of a break. Let's say initially she charged $50 an hour, with the first session totally free. When she began to employ the second model, she raised her hourly rate to $70 with the first half hour free and the second half hour costing $35. She took a $15 cut in hourly rate, but managed to hang on to her business and her clientele until a better economy returned.

Eventually she went to a system of $1 a minute and let the clients decide between a half hour ($30), a full hour ($60), or an hour and a half ($90). This strategy represented a "comfort" fee that we'll get to in a minute, but let's talk about the economy first.

In addition to the sources listed at the beginning of this chapter, the national (and local) economies also play a large role in determining how much you can charge for fees, and even economic experts have trouble predicting what will happen in local markets at any given time. When money is tight and people are not spending much on luxuries, things like a nice, soothing massage, or a body-calming yoga class can get crossed off the list as non-essential. Therefore, it is good to get in the habit of saving money for these times, to pay attention to the economic indicators, and to figure out how you would cope if your clientele suddenly, or even gradually, dropped off.

What are the economic indicators? The cost of housing is a big one. If house prices in your area are skyrocketing, it's a good indicator that the economy is doing pretty well. On the other hand, if those high-priced houses are sitting on the market too long (over six months), it's probably an indication that the market is slowing down. Housing "starts" are another indicator: if a lot of new houses are going up it's good, but the opposite connotes bad news for the economy.

Another indicator is the Dow Jones average, which is broadcast on the news every night. You don't need to be an expert on stock fluctuations, and you don't have to scan the fine print for individual shares in the newspaper, to understand what certain numbers mean. If it is announced that the Dow Jones average has dropped one or two thousand points below 13,000 (as of 2007), that means that the market is down. If it is 13,000 or above, that means the market is doing well. These figures represent the value of selected stocks traded in a given period of time, usually a day. If the value of stocks traded is up, it represents confidence on the part of investors in the likelihood of the market remaining "healthy" for a while. If the values of stocks drop, it means investors are sensing a downturn in the market. Another indicator of what's happening in the market is the Consumer Confidence Index (CCI), which can be found in your local newspaper, or on the Internet at www.conference-board.org/economics/ConsumerConfidence.cfm. This index projects the likelihood of consumers spending more or less money on goods and services, given their perception of the market. If the job market is not good, and consumers are uncertain and concerned about the economy, the CCI will take a downturn.

These figures do not need to rule your life, but for business owners, it would be foolhardy to ignore the obvious indicators of economic trouble brewing. Think of your practice as belonging to a much larger system of market activities in the same way you think of your patients in a holistic way.

Sliding Scale Fee

Let's say you're well on your way, and seem to be having some regular success bringing in your clients. You live in a college town and you want to make your service available to students who have less money to spend on massage. A sliding fee scale allows you to offer your services at a lower rate for segments of the population who clearly do not have the resources to pay your regular rate. Although this sounds fairly simple it can be tricky. How do you know if the person really can't afford your rates?

You are not about to ask for a tax return to figure this out. Two categories of the population that merit a break are students and seniors. Obviously, not all students are broke, and many seniors have millions squirreled away, but because you can't know their financial background, you cannot assume anything. It's also just as likely that students don't have a lot of money, and it's a fact that many seniors are living on a fixed income and don't have a lot to spare. So, what you want to do is arrive at a blanket reduction for these two categories of clients. You will have to do some research on this to find out what is reasonable. Watch for specials in the paper placed by your competitors, and talk to your friends, relatives, and colleagues about what seems fair.

In addition to students and seniors, there may be others in the chronological middle who would love to come for your services, but legitimately can't handle your fees. What you decide in this instance may depend on your financial situation at the time. If someone comes in for a free session, and says they would love to come back, but they just can't afford it, what do you do? You're a kind-hearted soul and this client seems genuinely in need. A ready answer, one that is easily understood by everyone, is—that since time is money—go for the $1 a minute response. This allows everyone to participate. Furthermore, it is always your call if you have a cancer patient with high medical bills to reduce your fee as low as you want to go for that individual. What you want to watch out for is the perception that you are willing to do this for *every* client. The other thing to avoid is the perception that your policies are haphazard—made up on the spot.

Sit down and go through every scenario you can imagine regarding situations that could raise questions about your fees and policies. And, again, know them like the back of your hand. You don't want to wait until someone walks in the door to figure any of this out.

Remember that when you are just starting out, two clients a week may seem like a lot, but once you have worked on a total of 100 clients, you may soon realize that five clients a day is not hard at all for you. Everyone gets the jitters with the first few clients. Everyone says or does something they wish they hadn't in those first few sessions, but don't allow this to bring you down. Keep the number 100 in mind, and notice how you feel once you've reached that number. Confidence builds over time, but it really doesn't take that long to feel at home in your office, at ease with your clients, and satisfied that your business is chugging along just fine.

Eventually you'll want to raise your rates. You can usually raise your rates safely once a year to between 10% and 15% over your current rate. If you're charging $50 an hour, you can move up to $55 or even $60. In either case, you need to have a very good feel for what is happening in your local market. There was a period of time when I was unable to raise my ad rates for five years. When I started out in business, there was little competition, and I enjoyed the unique position of owning one of only two holistic health publications in my area. Then, suddenly, a new magazine appeared, and then another. Had I raised my rates at that time, I would have risked losing many of my clients, and perhaps the business itself.

Invoicing and Collections

For many holistic practices, it is assumed that payment is made at the time of the visit to the practitioner. This would be the case for most massage therapists, but not necessarily the case for chiropractors, psychotherapists, or anyone else who may be receiving payments from an insurance company. In these cases, you are most likely going to be sending an invoice either directly to the client or to the insurance company.

What exactly is an invoice? An invoice is a document that describes any products or services for which the buyer (in this case your client) is responsible for payment to the seller (you, who sold your services to your client). Invoice forms can be set up through your database management software. This software should enable you to call up all the names of the clients who owe you money and produce individual invoices, which you can then mail to your clients for payment.

The invoice should include your name, the name of your business, your business address, your business phone, fax, and email address. Remember that it is to your advantage to enable your clients to get in touch with you through a variety of media. The invoice will also include the date the service was performed (or the date the products were purchased), the hourly rate for the service, any amount of tax on the service, and the total. An invoice should also include a date by which the payment is due—usually within 30 days, but this is entirely up to you. It is also extremely helpful to include a separate envelope for the client to use to return payment. Nine times out of ten this will ensure a faster turn-around time.

Your word processing software should enable you to print individual envelopes which could be very helpful if your practice is small. Usually the envelopes have to be fed into a printer by hand, but this saves the additional cost of self-stick labels and the time it takes to apply them. On the other hand, it is faster to print labels, and if you sit in front of the TV some night doing the labeling, it goes by pretty quickly. The tricky thing here is to make sure that you are paying careful attention when matching up the invoice with the label. If you are only one client "off," you can end up sending Barbara Brant's invoice to Sam Clark, and so on down the line.

There are mailing houses that will do the stuffing and labeling for you, but I do not advise you to use them initially. They are expensive and you will forego your chance to make sure that each invoice is correct. I found enough mistakes I had made in tallying ad charges, or even miniscule typos, to realize that I needed to have personal control over what went out of my office and what did not.

Many of my clients, and no doubt yours too, have unusual names or common names with unusual spellings. In the holistic community, where we are skilled at seeing the individual human being and appreciating his or her unique qualities, names have a special importance. Make sure you get the client's name down correctly the first time. Don't hesitate to ask them how to spell their name. The name "Kate" could be spelled "Cate" and you would never know unless you asked. After the client leaves, double-check the spelling of the person's name on your computer where you have stored him or her in your database management software. If you get it right the first time, you can rest easily. Most likely all invoicing and other print materials that issue from that program will be correct thereafter. See Figure 6-1 for a sample invoice.

As I mentioned in an earlier chapter, coping with the lack of payment can be a drag. A rate of 10 percent for non-payment is not unusual, so assume that at least some of your folks are not going to pay you, and that another group of them will drag their feet in doing so. That's just the way it is; it's not just a phenomenon in the holistic community.

When someone fails to pay you by your deadline, you should first call him or her by phone and leave a message if necessary. If you don't get a response, send them a gentle reminder in the mail. You may think this is a little too soft an approach, but there are many legitimate reasons that people do not pay you on time—or at least reasons that you could understand. For example, someone might be away on vacation, or they have had to deal with an unexpected family crisis, or they may be going through an ugly divorce, or they may be reeling from a recent diagnosis of serious illness. You just have no way of knowing, so you don't want your first reaction to be one of anger or aggression.

If your first letter does not elicit a response, send another one with a more stern tone. If that letter doesn't get a rise out of your client, send the final one with a copy to your lawyer. This covers you if legal action becomes a possibility. If you indicate that a copy has been sent to your lawyer, you must actually send one to him or her. You may want to send this letter by registered mail because your receipt serves as a legal document if you should ever decide to go after a client in court.

In this third letter, you want to reiterate your payment policies, your willingness to work on a mutually satisfying financial arrangement, and your availability to be contacted. If at the end of this process, you still get no response, you may have no choice but to resort to hiring a collections agency or to taking legal action. My guess is that this will depend a great deal on your willingness to

Figure 6-1.

The invoice below is an example of an invoice I used when billing my clients. It contains the essential information for my business, as well as the current charges, monies already received for the previous billing, and the remaining total owed.

Your Business Name Here

100 Main Street
Healthville, USA 00000
333/555-0000

INVOICE

The current date goes here.

Name of the Business
First Name, Last Name
Street Address
City, State,   Zip

CHARGES			Charges	Received	Balance
$120.00	Logo(s)	Fall 07	$135.00		$135.00
	Display(s)	Summer '07	$135.00	$135.00	
$15.00	Calendar	Spring 07			
	Classifieds	Winter '06			
	Reset				
	Halftone (Photo)				
	XWords/XSpace	PAST DUE	$0.00	TOTAL	$135.00
	Internet				
$135.00	TOTAL				

MasterCard or Visa Number

___-___-___-___

Expiration Date _____

Payment is due upon receipt of this invoice. Payments received after 30 days
from the date listed above will incur an interest charge of ?%.

follow through, and the dollar amount that is owed. If the sum is substantial, talk to your lawyer about what to expect in a legal suit. What are your chances of recovering some, or all, of the payment owed? How long will it take? What do you need to do in order to make this happen?

See Figure 6-2 for an example of a dunning letter.

Going back to that first phone call you've made for obtaining payment, let's say a client returns your call, promises to make the payment and then fails to do so—again. What should you do? Try to reach them again by phone and get the *real* reason they are not paying. You can do this without asking personal questions. You can simply say that you understand hard times can happen, remind the client that he or she did promise to make a payment and then failed to do so—so what's up? You can say *you* are feeling confused—that maybe *you* didn't understand what they had said in that first phone call. You knew perfectly well what they said, but this gives them a chance to explain their actions. Ask if there is a way you can work with them to solve the problem. If they still promise to pay and don't, they are either terribly embarrassed by their circumstances (which may, in fact, be grim), or just plain unscrupulous. Fortunately, the latter folk are few and far between. Unless there is a large sum of money involved, bless them on their way and be glad to see them go.

Billing Insurance Companies

Dealing with insurance claims filed by your clients for payment to you (third party payments) can be frustrating and time-consuming. An insurance company may deny coverage for one patient, but grant it for another—even when both hold the same policy. Or they may deny a perfectly legitimate claim because of an incorrect code number. Individual companies differ greatly in terms of what they will and won't cover. Some practitioners go into business thinking they can solve the problem of insurance company reimbursements by insisting that their clients pay them directly. Under this arrangement, the client then asks the insurance company to reimburse them for the money they have had to pay to a practitioner. This notion is

Figure 6-2.

ANY SMALL BUSINESS
123 Main Street
Anytown, US 12345

Monday, November 29, 2004

Dear Eileen:

Your account is past due. We know sometimes it can be difficult to juggle accounts and we want to accommodate our advertisers as much as possible. Unfortunately your failure to respond to our invoices has gone beyond reasonable time limits.

Non-payment of your contract hurts small businesses like ours. We agreed to publish your ad based on your commitment to pay your bill when it arrived. Payment is not dependent on whether or not you receive responses to the ad. It is dependent on whether you requested an ad and whether the ad appeared in the magazine.

We are willing to recognize a "good faith" agreement and would welcome your efforts to set up a fair schedule of repayment if you are truly experiencing hardship. Most likely you are receiving this letter because we have not heard *anything* from you. If you do not pay the enclosed bill within thirty days, or call our office to make definite arrangements for repayment, we will have to turn your account over to collections. We do not want to take this step, and we strongly encourage you to contact us immediately.

Yours truly,
Polly Baumer
Publisher

cc: Douglas Anderson, atty.
Third notice

---

naive at best since many clients don't have the money to pay your fee. In fact, most clients will make a determination as to whether they'll come to you or not based on what insurances you accept. Whether you charge $50 an hour or $130 an hour, the number of people who are willing, or able, to pay you directly, may not keep you in business.

For many practitioners, the largest portion of income will come through an insurance company because of claims filed by your clients. Therefore, it behooves you to know as much as possible about how this claim process works, and to establish good working relationships with your insurance companies. Typically a practitioner becomes "paneled" by an insurance company as an in-network provider of care. This means that a particular insurance company recognizes you, the practitioner, as a legitimate provider who conforms to the insurance company's educational and experiential requirements. Most psychotherapists, for example, are on several insurance panels such as Blue Cross/Blue Shield, and Harvard Pilgrim. Because it can be difficult to become paneled as a sole proprietor with little or no experience, many practitioners will start out working for an established group practice. In this way, they become paneled automatically as a member of that group, and even if they leave the group later, they can usually become paneled as a sole proprietor on their own after that.

Because of their caring nature, practitioners seem to be more interested in providing for their clients than they do in filling out the appropriate insurance forms. With the proliferation of healthcare institutions, such as health maintenance organizations (HMOs), preferred provider organizations (PPOs), and independent practice associations (IPAs), plus Medicare and Medicaid, the healthcare industry has become very crowded and complex. Other factors that complicate the picture include changing government regulations, pressure from insurance companies to justify the need for care, reduced reimbursements, and more cases of insurance fraud. In addition, a law passed in the late 1990s, the Health Insurance Portability and Accountability Act (HIPAA), which addresses the privacy of healthcare records, can actually render a practitioner guilty of noncompliance if they fail to attend a seminar, or hire a consultant, to learn the proper way to obtain (and protect) medical information from a client.

Another headache is coping with claim denials, which often results in having to resubmit a claim as many as three times before receiving reimbursement. Unfortunately, sorting out all these details can result in a huge amount of time spent by the individual therapist. Failing to figure it out, however, can result in long delays in reimbursement, or no reimbursement at all, from insurance companies.

Workman's compensation claims make up a significant number of insurance reimbursement requests. Regulated by individual states, workman's compensation claims are navigated through state bureaucracies, and can be easily rejected if the procedures required are not followed to the letter. You need to identify the appropriate office in your state, and ask for a written copy of their procedures.

Personal injury claims offer yet another form of reimbursement, but these can be the most difficult since they often involve court cases that may go against the insured. This means you will not be reimbursed by your client's insurance company if you have been treating the client prior to a judgment. You could see someone for a full year before even knowing if you'll ever get paid.

To adequately cope with the requirements of the insurance companies, the laws of your state, and the various healthcare institutions, it is advisable for beginners to spend the money (which you can include as part of your business plan) on a one-time session with a healthcare consultant, or an all-encompassing seminar, on these subjects. This will be money well spent, and if you do it at the beginning, you can set up all your systems for bookkeeping and recordkeeping to conform to what you will need for compliance. Changes to the laws and changes to insurance coverage are inevitable, but it is much easier to make incremental adjustments to your process, than to have to start from scratch. Remember that you want to create for yourself the easiest, most user-friendly, method of tracking data so that you don't have to spend more than a few minutes a day doing it. A place to start would be Consultants in Counseling Practice Management (at counseling-privatepractice.com) for psychotherapists, and Open Directory-Healthcare Management (at dmoz.org/Business/Healthcare/Healthcare_Management/Consulting/) for other practitioners. Also check with your Chamber of Commerce for someone local who may be experienced, so you don't have to pay to travel.

What you want to learn from a consultant is how to set up your bookkeeping and recordkeeping for clients so that you can easily extract information needed for insurance companies. You need to find out what to do in order to comply with the state and federal laws governing insurance claims, and you need to ask questions about how the insurance industry works. How do you file a claim? What is a reasonable time for a response from the insurance company? Why are claims typically denied? Can you resubmit after a denial? How many times? What can you do to hasten the process? What insurance companies are best suited to your practice, and which ones should you avoid? Will insurance companies cover your work at two separate offices?

Even seasoned therapists who have been in practice for years can find dealing with insurance claims daunting. Just know that it can be done, and that since it is the primary way you will receive income, you need to study it carefully.

As you can see from the number of considerations that accompany insurance claims, the paperwork can easily pile up, and the time for assessing when payments are due can slip by. Make a note of when each payment should be due from the insurance company and place it in your tickler file. Do a little insurance-related paperwork every day so that it doesn't buildup into a mountain.

Summary

Use market indicators and your knowledge of other therapists in your area to determine your fee. Think about how, or if, you would apply a sliding scale fee. Prepare a strategy for invoicing and collecting monies owed to you, and create a form letter in advance. Establish a good working relationship with an individual at each of the insurance companies who accept your billing. Hire a consultant, or attend a seminar, in order to learn exactly how insurance billing works, and what you need to do to comply with company policy and the law. Don't let insurance paperwork build up—have a calendar or tickler file for following up on payments that are due.

CHAPTER SEVEN

Everything is Marketing– Marketing is Everything

Now that you are a business owner, you are ready for the golden rule of sales: everything is marketing; marketing is everything. This means that your every word, thought, and action has an impact on your business. When your first client walks in the door, you want to exude confidence, and welcome him with enthusiasm, because you know you are going to help this person, and that he is going to be very happy with the result. This is the absolute beauty of holistic health. You already know it isn't all about the money. You do want to set in motion a constant exchange of energy and goodwill that brings clients back again and again, and that fosters your own job satisfaction. This effort requires constant vigilance on your part in order for you to give each client the same amount of care and attention.

A Practice Session

Imagine that your first client has just walked into your office. He's perused the reading material in your waiting room, quickly scanned the décor and your desk, what does he focus on now? Yes, you, the practitioner. What would you like him to see in this person? For starters, warmth. As a holistic health practitioner, you want to greet all your clients with a presence that says, "I honor the divine within you. Welcome to my sanctuary." A smile virtually always assures newcomers. Make sure you are not harried when your client arrives. Plan your schedule so that you automatically build in a five-minute period to meditate quietly before each patient arrives. To that add another five minutes for scanning his record and familiarizing yourself with his medical and personal details.

Ask the client to come in and have a seat. Walk him through your medical form, explaining what it is for, and how you intend to use it. (See Appendix B for sample questions to ask on intake forms.) Have a pen ready for him to complete the form. You may want to start by asking him whether he's ever been to a massage therapist, or an acupuncturist, before. If so what was his experience? Why did he go to one and did he receive relief for his condition? This is not meant to be an interrogation, but a friendly way of obtaining information about the client, not the least of which will come through body language. Is the client nervous? Does he seem rushed himself? How does he respond to your questions? The author of *Blink*, an experienced business and science reporter, claims that people "think without thinking"—that they form their impressions of something, or someone, in the blink of an eye. You have precious little time to put the client at ease and assure him of your competence, so make the very most of it. I find that most holistic practitioners do this automatically and very well. Remember that it is of the utmost importance to instill trust in your client. Be respectful of whatever they are putting forth, and try to get to know them as a human being, not just a body on the table.

What Can the Client Expect?

This is where you can really shine. You know your craft intimately and you can explain what you are going to do. If you are a chiropractor and your client has never been to one before, you can explain that it is not necessary to remove your clothing—a big relief to many people—and that the Three Stooges actually began as chiropractors. Just kidding!

I went to a chiropractor for the first time after I injured my neck in a badminton accident. My head flew back as I went for a shot and I had a stiff neck for two weeks. Then three. Then six. Finally I decided to try chiropractic because I'd heard such wonderful things about it. Sure enough, just like in the Three Stooges movies, the chiropractor took my head and swiveled it around to the sound of several cracks. It was all over in a second, and my neck was instantly better, but I do remember being stunned and a little shaken by that first experience.

My point is simply that if you are very clear with your new clients about what you are going to do, and when you are going to do it, you can allay their fears and help them become participants in their own healing. If you are a psychotherapist, and your client has never been in therapy, an explanation from you about your process would be tremendously helpful. In your case, it may be harder to begin because people are reluctant to tell their stories, let alone their deepest secrets to a stranger. Anything you can do or say to make them feel more comfortable is a progressive step.

Along those lines, any history you can briefly describe about your craft can be helpful. When Dr. Samuel Hahneman first established homeopathy, it must have seemed ludicrous to his patients. Homeopathic pills contain a distillation of water with the smallest possible amount of a curative element, yet they are amazingly effective. Homeopathy is enormously popular in Britain and Europe, but until the last decades of the 20th century, it has been viewed almost like voodoo in the U.S. You, as a practitioner, may have to go to extra lengths to explain how your profession operates, and what results can be expected.

To fully prepare for your clients, it may be helpful to think about what *you* might ask a therapist if you were going to one for the first time. Typical questions for a psychotherapist might be:

1. What is your hourly rate?

2. Do you charge an interview fee?

3. What is your educational training?

4. How long have you been a therapist?

5. What types of therapy do you practice?

6. Do you have a sliding scale fee?

7. What is your cancellation policy?

8. Do you keep written records?

9. Who is allowed to see those records?

10. Do you offer phone sessions?

11. Are you available for a phone call in a crisis?

12. Has a malpractice suit ever been filed against you?

You should be prepared to answer many other questions as well, including questions regarding your ethical practices, whether or not you receive regular supervision, whether you attend additional classes to stay current in your field, and what professional organizations you belong to. You may even get some very personal questions, which you'll have to answer at your own discretion. Try to anticipate curveballs that may be thrown in your direction. Ask another practitioner in your field to put you through the wringer in order to cover as much ground as possible in advance.

Let's say you've now completed your imaginary session with your client, and he is about to leave. Let him take as much time as he needs to refocus. After a massage, or a strenuous psychotherapy session, it may take a few minutes for some people to enter the "real world" again. Have you set up his next appointment? Never rush a client out the door, and when possible, walk them out. Personal touches make a difference. What you want them to know, and what they want you to show, is that you care about them.

Answering Your Phone

Clients who come to you by word-of-mouth will have gotten an indication of what you are like from the person recommending you. But what about the people who see your ad in the Yellow Pages or the newspaper? If someone is calling because of your ad, it means your first *visual* impression was a good one, that is, the first visual representation of your business in printed material. Now what?

When you pick up the phone to answer it, this is your chance to make a first *audio* impression, but your second chance to seal the deal. Most likely when you are starting out you won't have a secretary, so what does your message say? Is it clearly audible? Your message should sound friendly, professional, and enthusiastic without going overboard. You'll want to state clearly what your hours are, and how soon the caller can expect a return call. It's okay to put your own personal "stamp" on your message, but check it out with friends and family members before you make a final decision about how you want to come across. What you say and do here is critical because your answering system is your lifeline to your livelihood. If the message is a turn-off, you can expect to hear someone hanging up. Don't wait for that to happen three times before changing your message.

Furthermore, you should never slam the phone down. This seems so obvious, but I know a number of people who do this without ever realizing the effect it has on the caller. In addition, you shouldn't leave your answering machine on speaker mode when another client is present. I know it's hard to believe, but I've been in at least two offices where this has been the case. No one wants to think that they are addressing a room full of your other clients when they call you.

Whether you are using a machine or the phone system to record your calls, your system needs to be flexible so that your message can be changed easily every day if needed. How reliable is it? How often do you check it?

Here is where I recommend you spend some money because in the end it will result in real savings. I used to have an answering machine. The tape would stop, or get stuck and I was not in the office to fix it. Voices would often be garbled. I would miss calls, and people would call up days later and ask why I hadn't answered their calls. Invest in your local call answering service. It costs about $12.00 a month and is worth every penny. You will never miss calls, you can change the message easily, and you can retrieve messages from another phone down the street, or out of town, if necessary.

You should check out all the phone services that your phone company offers because these features can make your life much simpler. Some of them will not be necessary for your business, but others can prove quite valuable. If you get a million calls from marketing companies or fund-raisers not covered under the Do Not Call Act, you can pay a small fee to permanently block those numbers. If you do opt for call forwarding, I would not interrupt a call with a client to take another call. This practice is so annoying. It's one thing if it's an emergency, but none of us is very good at gauging just how long we are conversing with someone *else* after saying, "Oh, excuse me for a minute. I have another call." Remember, there are also *other* therapists and your client may soon be going to them instead.

Returning Calls

Returning calls is a habit you will get into right away. It isn't even hard if you think of each call as a potential deposit in your bank account. When I was running my magazine, I relied very heavily on my phone answering service, especially at deadline time. I tried to monitor my calls three times a day, in the morning, at lunchtime, and at the end of the day. I was working with as many as 200 people for any given issue of my magazine, and I needed the frequent contact so that I could determine which calls were the most urgent to address and which ones could wait. Even so, I tried never to let more than 24 hours go by before returning a call. There were times when I got 50 calls a day, so I was very happy when that last call was made.

One of the frustrations of any business is the demanding nature of some of your clients. Most people are very courteous and understand when you don't return their calls immediately, but there are the other few who can't seem to understand how you could let an hour go by without calling them back. A good rule of thumb here is to use your instincts and try as much as possible to get back to your clients as soon as you can. It's much easier to make a few calls at noon and a few at the end of the day, instead of waiting to make all of them the next morning, but if that works for you, great. Just make sure that too much time has not passed between the call and its return.

If you are going out of town, your message should indicate that you will not be in your office. A note of caution here, however. Sometimes, even though your message says you are not available, the answering service will allow clients to leave a message anyway. This is confusing to your clients because it can sound like you really *will* call them back even though you're in Aruba. Just say in your message that even though they may be asked to leave a message at the end of the call, you will not be returning any calls until your return, and provide them with the date of your return. Most clients will not leave messages under this condition.

Email

Email is an increasingly popular way for you to reach your clients and for them to reach you. It can be an inexpensive way to announce specials, gift certificates, and any promotions you are running. It can also be very difficult to have to respond to too many emails. Here is where a straightforward written policy regarding email can be very helpful. Ask your clients if they would like to receive notices of your promotions through email. Explain to them that when you are unable to return email because you are out of town or otherwise unavailable, they will receive an automatic message to that effect if they try to contact you through email. You can also clearly state the types of email requests you are comfortable responding to and those you are not. This could be very helpful to psychotherapists, who could easily be inundated with email requests from clients with problems. Just because people can reach you, and just because they want your attention to their needs, does not mean you must respond in every possible way. You are in charge here. You can set the boundaries and it's important that you do so.

Dealing With People

To me, dealing with people offers both the best and the worst aspects of any business. Fortunately, by far the greatest number of people I interacted with through interviews, advertising, and business schmoozing, were truly lovely and this is one of the more fabulous things about working in the holistic community. But for some reason, this community of caregivers also seems to attract a small number of people who just can't—or won't—cope or cooperate. Although these people can be very frustrating, you can usually find a

way to work with them. I think of them as falling into three categories: the talkers, the complainers, and the overwhelmed. We'll get to
them in a minute.

For the most part, if you regularly employ positive affirmations,
you will begin to realize that you are attracting exactly the type of
clientele you want. When your clients appreciate you and you, in
turn, appreciate them, something larger begins to grow. Call this
process the metaphysics of business. Good energy begets more good
energy, and the whole thing snowballs into a wonderfully blossom-
ing practice. It's good to remember this concept at some point during each day, but particularly after a session with one of your more
problematic clients.

The Talkers

The talkers you can't do much about—it's their hour and they're
paying for it, so if it bothers you, you just have to make sure you
mentally soothe yourself after they leave. I find excessive talkers completely exhausting. You just have to hope they are good storytellers.
You also have to understand these people are, for whatever reason,
very uncomfortable with silent places in a conversation, and that
their habit of speaking incessantly may be providing something they
need, sort of like a security blanket. Sometimes this stems from anxiety that can be masked by a very outgoing and confident personality.
If the talking truly interferes with your work, you may want to address it directly, and ask the client not talk while you are doing this
or that, or for the next fifteen minutes because you are going to do—
whatever—and you need their full concentration.

Talking is also something practitioners need to be aware of for
themselves. You don't want to be guilty of taking up all the audible
space in the room with someone who just came in for a quiet, relaxing massage. This can be a real challenge for serious yakkers, but it's
one of the reasons people will not return. If you want a steady clientele, mum's the word. Well, of course, you can talk a *little*, but be
aware of whether or not you're overwhelming your clients. Remember, too, that everything you say matters, so never, ever gossip or
criticize other people. Doing so makes you look small, and it never

accomplishes anything worthwhile. You also want to avoid getting too far out there on the metaphysical plane in conversation with your more traditional clients. I heard about a feldenkrais practitioner who was elated to get a call from a radiologist wanting a solution to his chronically stiff neck. This practitioner was also an astrologer, and started talking to the radiologist about his horoscope while she was working on him. He abruptly got up in the middle of the session and left! Stick to your boundaries.

The Complainers

Complainers may have had controlling parents—or at least one controlling parent—who knows, but they have a hard time allowing comfort and peace into their psyches. Holistic healers make a place even for these folks. Besides, they may need your services more than anyone else. Although they complain constantly, and convey that nothing is ever good enough or quite right, they will return again and again. If this happens, you may have enabled it. Here's how: in your quest for presenting your most pleasant and enthusiastic self, you have unwittingly invited them to test your limits. Your kindness and patience is the fuel for their fire, or, I should say, ire. This plays out with the client first presenting himself or herself as genial, then slowly disintegrating into a pain in the neck, whining over the roughness of your touch. Eventually they may start criticizing your techniques, which they claim have left them bruised and sore. The pleasure such clients enjoy from ridiculing you, and no doubt many others in their lives, is beyond my understanding, but I've experienced the phenomenon often enough to recognize it fairly soon after meeting one of these folks.

One way to cope with these people is to say directly, without anger or malice, "You seem to be troubled by my the way I do my work. Perhaps another practitioner would better serve you. I understand that I cannot accommodate the needs of all clients." Period, the end. Maybe they will stay and behave more civilly, or maybe they will leave and never come back. That's okay. It's true that you cannot please everyone, but what's important is that you did not exhibit behavior you would regret later. Instead, you handled yourself very professionally, and placed the ball in the client's court. What I like about this approach is that it's totally honest and allows the practitioner, usually a very caring person, to stand up for herself or himself. You must be able to do this if you are going to be successful in business.

I had one client, someone who advertised with me for years, who *always* blew up before he cooled down. His very first reaction over the phone if anything was amiss with his ad, was to come on like a Sherman tank, just madder than hell. The first two times this happened, I confess I got very upset myself, but had to keep it together so as not to yell back, or, worse, burst into tears. The third time he called, I sat at the other end of the phone idly twirling the cord until his tantrum ran its course, and then we discussed his reason for calling. So, not all complainers are people you want to eliminate from your practice. You just have to know how to handle them. This is a skill you will develop over time. Understand that the complainers of this world have far greater problems in their lives than you and your techniques. Your service to them may well be in soothing their own underlying fear of failure.

The flip side of this is what to do when you are at fault. I had a client who called me up to say that he was unhappy about the way his ad had appeared in the magazine. He said, "You charged me $250, and I don't think that's fair!" Instead of reverting to my pricing policies, which I knew backwards and forwards, I simply said, "Well, talk to me. What do *you* think is fair?" I didn't say it in anger or with any kind of sarcasm, and he knew that. My tone allowed him to feel that he was being heard, which he was. Rather than insist that the ad infraction was very minor and would not affect his responses, I simply adjusted the price and let it go. It may have cost me $20, but it was worth it. He advertised with me for over ten years. He knew that if he had a problem, we could discuss it, and come to an arrangement that suited us both.

Flexibility is essential to negotiations with your clients. It may take a while before you get a feel for what you can compromise on and what you can't, but the perception on the part of your clients that you are willing to compromise is worth it's weight in gold.

Going back to our complainers, another less direct way to elimi-nate them is simply to explain that you are booked well into the next millennium. Sometimes people just want a target and you could be it. Again, how you deal with this is entirely up to you, but be careful because what the client *says* about how you dealt with him is—yep, marketing.

The Overwhelmed

As a new practitioner, one of the things to watch for when meet-ing a client for the first time is what their body language is telling you. Eye contact is the first thing to look for. Is the client looking at your face or staring at the floor as she talks? Are her eyes darting around the room? Is she fidgeting? There are many reasons people might avoid your gaze. Some people are just shy, others nervous, and still others may be coping with emotional issues such as a recent death, marital problems, a traumatic accident—any number of things. Less common are clients who may have a history of not feeling safe with strangers because of abuse or neglect. Any of these clients may be emotionally fragile, so handle with care. Your job is to provide them with a safe, clean, and comfortable setting; and treat them with respect and dignity.

Your training has probably prepared you for the client for whom massage unexpectedly evokes a sad memory. (This can happen in many other disciplines as well.) The client may begin to cry. This might be the response you would expect of someone who is grieving and depressed, but what if it happens to Mr. Bank President who just came in for a lunch-hour pick-me-up. Do you know how to handle it? They way you proceed with this dilemma could travel the phone lines. If the school from which you graduated did not address this possibility, it would be worth it for you to seek professional ad-vice on how to cope if this should ever occur. It's not likely, but there could be legal and professional implications if you handle it badly. At the very least you will want to give the person some space to get themselves back together, and assure them that bodywork often trig-gers memories locked in the tissues that have long since been forgot-ten. It is a positive thing to have them released.

Needless to say, you do not want to act shocked, horrified or panic-stricken. Allow your humanity to prevail and you will do just fine. Here is where the concept of "as if" comes in very handy. Even if you haven't the vaguest clue as to what to do in this case (or any other situation related to your business), act "as if" you did. Your clients want to believe that you know exactly what you're doing no matter what. This does not mean that you should lie or cheat. It simply means that in order to reach the top level of performance in your craft, you must apply the utmost professionalism, demonstrating integrity and compassion. If you are not licensed to give advice, don't give any, but you can always demonstrate kindness and concern. Ask if there are issues your client would like you to understand before proceeding any further.

Finally, when the client is out the door and you're asking yourself, "Will they come back?" you want to be able to reflect on the session, and know that you gave it your best effort. If you think you didn't, try to identify what might have gone wrong, and think about how you might prevent it from happening in the future. This error could be anything from not being attentive enough to your client, not speaking when you were spoken to—the list is long. Don't beat yourself up over it; we all make mistakes. Just remember that repeat business is very important, and that the vast majority of your comments, techniques, and actions must speak to a certain level of expertise in order to have clients return again and again.

Know Your Policies

When I first started working on my magazine, I was working with policies and prices that I inherited from the previous publishers. I was very grateful for having a framework for determining how much any given ad would cost, but this system of pricing was not easy to understand. Although it made sense from a business standpoint in terms of making a profit, it was often hard to explain to other people unfamiliar with the industry. The cost of advertising did not depend solely on the size of an ad. In some cases it depended on the number of words included in the ad. On top of that there could be an additional charge for ads that ran over the word count, and the specified size. In the beginning, I often got tripped up when I would try to explain this complicated structure to my advertisers.

Eventually I understood why it had been set up the way it had, and how the system paid for the magazine and a salary for me. Still it was enormously complex, and I did have to go over it many times. Over time, the pricing changed to accommodate a more competitive market, but in the meantime, it was essential for me to know my policies well enough to be able to explain them clearly to my clients.

Once you have decided on your fee, you'll need to think about the policies you want to employ regarding cancellations, missed appointments, and any other issues that are likely to come up between you and a client. You should put these in writing and memorize them as if your life depended on them. If you enter into a disagreement with a client because of a cancellation, and that person gives you a hard time about paying for that session because the cancellation time was not within 24 hours of the appointment, you want to have something immediately available in your hand to indicate you set these policies up a long time ago. In other words, you don't want your clients to think you are simply making them up on the spot.

As we discussed in Chapter Four, when you make an appointment with a client, it is a good idea to give a very brief overview of your policies, and when possible, mail them out to the client before his or her appointment, so they have time to review them at home. Include the list of insurances you accept, and any arrangements you are willing to make for repayment if the client does not have insurance with any of those insurance companies. Do clients have to pay you at the time of the session or are you willing to send them a bill? If you send them a bill, you may want to increase the total slightly to cover the costs of printing the bill, the cost of the envelopes, the postage, and your time putting it all together.

Slow Pays

My magazine was only published every three months, so I bent over backwards to get the latecomers in. Deadline time was always such a rush that receiving payment right then and there was virtually impossible. And, yes, I did have people who never did pay, but there were very, very few of them. I also had a number of clients who did not pay immediately when the bill was due. This was a problem for me because it affected the cash flow I needed for the payment of my own bills for production, distribution, and a million other things.

I knew that many of my clients were very busy, and some were just disorganized, and that was why they were so slow in making payments. I finally decided to pay the cost of a return envelope that I included in their bill. All of a sudden, the payments were coming in on time. So, I spent a certain amount of money to hasten the process of bill paying, but it was well worth it because of the speed with which money returned to me.

Let's look at non-payment further. As I mentioned earlier, very few people really fell into the deadbeat category. I would say it amounted to less than ten percent of my business. When figuring my budget, I always anticipated this figure and padded my costs accordingly. I was especially frustrated by the people who begged to be included in the magazine at the last minute and then did not pay. The worst of these was a trade show marketer who took out a half page ad worth about $500 and virtually disappeared afterward.

I looked into the cost of collections and the cost of taking people to small claims court and decided not to bother with either. If you choose the court route, you will have to file a lengthy document, and pay between $20 and $50 for the pleasure. Then, if you're lucky, you can expect to wait from six to nine months before the case ever goes to court. By that time in *my* life, I have moved on to other things. I decided not to go through collections because the individual amounts of money that people owed me were relatively small, but the fees charged by collection agencies were not.

I did, however, get a great deal of satisfaction from allowing people who owed me money, but who were genuinely experiencing hardship, to get off the hook completely. If I saw that a payment was late, I sent the first reminder with a pleasant note. The second reminder was more stern, and the third very clearly stated that we needed to set up a system of repayment; that I needed to hear from them immediately; and that failure to contact me *might* negatively affect their credit record. This was true. If I had reported their lack of payment to the Better Business Bureau, or worse, to the three credit agencies (Equifax, TransUnion and Experian), it could have been a black mark on their record.

The third letter usually extracted some kind of response from the client and I always made arrangements that were feasible for him or her ($10 a month if necessary). After a client sent in two of these miniscule payments, I would forgive the debt. I performed my own little two-minute ceremony, thanking the universe that I didn't have this problem anymore, and blessing the poor client who was clearly having a much tougher time than I making ends meet. I called the client to say I was forgiving the debt, and whether they were grateful or not, I didn't care at that point. There is no reason to cling to these situations. Just let them slide right on down the river and move on. If you can't, and you insist on extracting your pound of flesh, maybe you need to look at your own values a little more closely. It never makes a bigger person out of you to make someone else feel small.

As a business owner, you will constantly walk the line between fairness to yourself and fairness to your clients. At the end of the day, you want to be proud of your actions and you want to feel good about yourself. Depositing a steady stream of checks in the bank is great for your self esteem, but knowing that you have taken the high road in a difficult situation, and managed to come out unscathed, can be just as valuable spiritually. Sometimes that involves standing up for yourself as we said before, especially for sensitive, caring people who do not resonate with competitive bravado, but instead prefer a more cooperative and creative approach to problem solving.

On the other hand, if you find that the same client is working you (or your payment process) over repeatedly, and taking advantage of your good nature on a regular basis, you are welcome to refuse to see that client again. No pay, no way. Everyone understands this. Just make sure you handle it well.

You will also want to decide how you want to handle checks that bounce. What is the arrangement you have with your bank? How much will you charge your client for the problem? Will you give them another chance with another check, or will you insist on cash or a money order? Be sure to include your final answer in your policy statement.

Working With Vendors

Your vendors are the people who provide you with services: the laundry that washes your sheets, the person who plows the snow off the driveway for you, or rakes the leaves off the office lawn, your mail carrier, the UPS person—all are the vendors of services to you. All of these people make your practice possible, so stay on good terms with them. If you get injured or become ill, they may be the ones who will help you maintain your practice. Make sure to learn their names, their usual times of arrival, and try to get to know them at least well enough to have a passing conversation every now and then. If you ever need them to perform a service for you with an especially rapid turn around time, you want to have a good working relationship with them. Establish business accounts with all the vendors who provide you with supplies, and get in the habit of paying their bills on time. If you run into a business slump and have a hard time repaying them, they will often make allowances for you as a regular customer.

Summary

Everything you do and say reflects on your business so make sure you have a pleasant message on your machine, and a handshake and smile for your clients. Get in the habit of returning phone calls regularly—don't let 24 hours go by before returning a call. Figure out a plan for handling the few clients whose behavior makes your day a challenge. Be prepared to discuss your policies clearly and in detail, and anticipate how you will deal with clients who are slow to pay you.

CHAPTER EIGHT

Spreading the Word– How to Advertise

Take a Day to Play

Once you have identified your hourly rate and policies, and conducted a practice session or two, you can start to think about who you are in business. The exercises that follow in this chapter are designed to help you get started. Have fun with them as you move along. I encourage you to take a day to play with your computer software and fiddle around with words and pictures.

Designing your own promotional materials can save you a lot of money, but even if you end up going to a professional graphic artist to produce your final products, it's very useful for you to do some playful homework in this area. If you become proficient enough, you may be able to produce things like business cards, brochures, and flyers yourself, saving time, money, and frustration in the end.

To do this you want to explore the options of your word processing program. Specifically you want to find a letter template and figure out how to use it to set up letters and letterheads of your own. You also want to figure out how to merge the names in your database management software with your word processing software so that you can create individual letters to your clients announcing any upcoming sales, gift certificates, or promotional items.

In addition, you want to play around with setting up the parameters of a business card, inserting a graphic, and creating special effects like shading. Graphics can be scanned into your computer via a scanner, downloaded from the Internet by way of clip art files, or imported from programs like Photoshop, Illustrator, and iPhoto. If you are using artwork that is not your own, be sure to check the copyright. Clip art is generally free of copyright infringement, but if you are using artwork that you've downloaded from the Internet, or culled from some other source, you want to make sure it is legal for you to use.

If you choose clip art, try to pick something that is not likely to be used by hundreds of other practitioners. Play around with spacing and direction. Photoshop and Illustrator are both excellent programs that allow you to flip, rotate or twist pictorial images. They will also allow for shading, sharpening, changing the contrast, and a wide variety of other artistic touches. If you don't have a program like Photoshop or Illustrator and can't afford one at this point, don't worry about it. Perhaps that will come later. You can always have someone design something for you initially, but fiddling with a few images on your own is very useful before you contact a professional. It will be a first step in figuring out how you want to present yourself. Some graphic artists charge by the job, others by the hour. If you have some idea ahead of time of what you would like to see in terms of your promotional materials, it will save you the cost of going back again and again to get it just right.

What's in an Ad?

Perhaps you have a lot of friends and relatives who want to avail themselves of your services. That's great for starters, but for a practice to continue with a steady stream of clients for years and years, you need to seek clients from a wider circle. Word-of-mouth is always good; a strategic advertising campaign can be even better and the results can last longer. Before you put yourself out there, you have to know who you are—at least who you are relative to your business. We're going to do a little exercise here that should help you define yourself and your practice.

The goal of advertising is to bring in clients and to establish yourself as a professional presence in your area. How do you do that?

Before you actually attempt to write anything down, it's important to ask yourself several questions.

1.   What makes your practice unique?

2.   What kind of clients do you want?

3.   How do you want to present yourself to the community?

This is a time for reflection. Thinking about what made you go into this business—what excited you in the first place about becoming a Reiki master—is key because your enthusiasm about your work must come through in your ad copy. Think about this as you answer the three questions above. You don't need to worry about whether you are creating the perfect ad; an advertising copywriter can do that for you, but you do need to be able to *tell* the copywriter what you want to say about yourself.

Who Are You?

Sit and think for a moment and then write down five qualities you possess that will aid you in your work. You may have 50 wonderful qualities, but try to identify the five you *know* will work in your favor. Examples would be:

> Good people skills
> Exceptional technique(s)
> Dependability
> Honesty
> Integrity
> Sense of Fairness
> Buoyancy—happy personality
> Practical
> Resourceful
> Forgiving
> Attentive
> Caring
> Kind
> Physically strong

Mentally sharp
Adaptable
Thoughtful
Eager to learn
Stoic
Not easily upset

Look back at the list and pat yourself on the back for your selections. Remember these are the areas where you *know* you shine, and they're the areas you'll want to emphasize somewhere in your promotional materials. This self-knowledge is very powerful. As long as it's truthful, you'll be able to stand behind these characterizations of yourself, and defend them without much effort when facing problems with your clientele. You'll be able to project them to your clients and *inject* them into your business. Read them again and think about how you might want to use these categories in an ad.

Now write down three qualities that you suspect will be a detriment to your practice—those things that might hold you back, or the things with which you'll have to struggle:

Procrastinator
Sloppy
Forgetful
Constantly running late
Easily offended, extra sensitive
Irritable
Short fuse
Talk too much
Too shy

Obviously, these are qualities you don't want to advertise. This is simply useful information for you. What came up almost immediately? For each of these negatives, you need to come up with creative solutions that will work for you. Let's say you're constantly running late. People expect to wait in a doctor's office, but they do not appreciate waiting for massage therapy, especially if they have taken time off from work on their lunch hour to do so. Force yourself to be on time by writing down the appointment time as 5 to 10 minutes earlier than you tell the client. If punctuality has been a chronic problem in your life, now is definitely the time to change that. Your family and friends may be willing to wait for you, but your clients will not. Lateness connotes a lack of concern for your clients' time, and a lack of organization on your part.

If you are a procrastinator, break your jobs down into doable pieces so that the work doesn't pile up. Pay the bills as they come in; don't wait until the end of the month. If you can get into the habit of doing several little things every day, it will make your life so much easier. I like to use the first hour of my working day getting my email and phone messages. Then I pay bills, return messages and *then* I do everything else. That way, the details are attended to right from the beginning, and I can devote myself to other tasks like editing or design.

Are you irritable? Overworked? Feeling rushed? If so, use the five-minute rule. Sit down in a comfortable chair and just relax for five minutes. It can make a big difference in how you feel and how you are likely to come across to one of your clients. These five minutes can seem like a long time, and although they really aren't, they can be very effective for this purpose.

Again, for each of your potential drawbacks, there is a way of coping. The important thing is to admit what the drawbacks are, and understand that you must figure out a way to work around them in order for your business to survive. You don't need to confide any of these things to anyone else, but you do need to address them as problems for yourself.

When I started out in business, I think my biggest negative trait was being overly sensitive to criticism. My friends would say to me, "Don't take it personally. It's just business." But I found that hard to accept since I *was* the business. That didn't last long, however. When you're alone in business, you have to "get over yourself" quickly. You soon learn that no matter how hard you try, you are going to make mistakes, but you can't let them slow you down. Just note them, learn from them, and move on. As I've described in other chapters, people often bring their problems to you, or take their frustrations out on you, but you must not let this get in the way of your success. Reread your positive attributes and take a moment to be thankful for them.

The Ad Text

After you've figured all this out, you're going to put together a brief introductory presentation. Now that you've thought about your own pros and cons, how are you going to introduce your service to the person on the street who is now holding your business card in his hand, or to an audience at a trade show? Imagine that you have only a couple minutes to explain what you do. Below are some examples. Read them carefully and figure out how you might apply a similar approach to your work. This will be the introduction you'll use if you're giving a lecture, talking to someone in line at the grocery store, or meeting a client for the first time. Obviously, you will have to tailor your presentation to the circumstances, but if you have a core sentence or two that you can reel out easily, this will help you get started. Eventually, the words will come very naturally.

Example 1:

Hello. I'm Nanette Hucknall, a career counselor and therapist. Do you know your true vocation in this life? Do you feel happy in your work? If not, it's never too late to make changes. Using visualization exercises to help you access your higher Self, the repository of your karmic biography, I take you through an "unlayering" process to move through fears and false belief systems to find your true vocation. You will:

- Discover the profession that will make you feel the most fulfilled.
- Encounter and work through blocks that could relate to childhood conditioning or past lives.
- Learn the best method to help you through negative belief systems.
- Develop a strategy that will lead you to your goal.

I am trained in Psychosynthesis, transpersonal psychology; have been a career therapist for six years; am the author of *Finding Your Work, Loving Your Life* published in 1992; and have 20 years of corporate management experience. I work with individuals and small groups; offer weekend intensives for out-of-towners; and workshops.

Example 2:

Hello. I'm Kippy Phelps, an expressive arts therapist. Expressive Arts Therapy (ET) intertwines creative arts modalities (art, music, dance, drama, creative writing) with verbal psychotherapeutic techniques. Accessing deep aspects of the psyche through image, sound, movement, metaphor, and story, ET offers new possibilities for emotional healing. As a healing catalyst, I listen with all six senses, facilitating the use of the expressive form most suited to the moment. Together, we co-create experiences that help you discover new ways to move through life-limiting obstacles. ET is particularly helpful in resolving body-related issues such as those stemming from abuse and trauma.

I offer individual, couples, family, and group therapy; supervision and consulting; expressive therapy and astrodrama workshops; and psychodrama groups.

I have a Masters degree in Expressive Therapies, and am currently completing advanced training in psychodrama. My work is grounded in 22 years of using the arts for personal and social change, and enriched by experience teaching in and learning from many cultures.

Example 3:

Hi. I'm Richard Shaw, a Rolfer. Rolfing is a method of working with the individual through the body. In a well-developed, ten-session series, the Rolfer, using fingers, palms, and arms, works slowly and gently with the connective tissue called "fascia" which holds together all the different parts of a person's body and gives that body its shape. For many reasons, from physical injury to emotional stress and trauma, our bodies develop areas which are less mobile, tight, and often painful. As the series progresses, these areas become freer, more open and stronger. These changes are lasting, and often dramatic and quite profound.

The more obvious results of Rolfing are: a person stands taller, is better supported, breathes more deeply and is more flexible and pain-free. The somewhat less obvious results are on the level of a person's own development. Rolfing is a work with great depth. We are working with imagination and care on areas of significance in a person's life.

A former dancer and teacher, I brought Rolfing to the Pioneer Valley area in 1985. Since then I have helped hundreds of people get out of pain as well as make important discoveries. I'm known for my gentle approach to this work, as well.

A free half-hour consultation is available to find out more about Rolfing and what kind of changes you could expect.

Did you notice how the speakers above gave a brief explanation of their craft, what a client could expect from it, and what their professional trainings are? Now let's move on to a written advertisement. We're going to keep the main text of the ad—that is everything but name, address, and phone number at the end—to about 120 words. This is a figure I work with a lot and have come to appreciate. It's just enough wording to cover what you need. From this initial attempt, we'll pare down the text for your business card and expand it for your brochure. Before you begin to write here are a few tips.

Rule #1: Do not refer to yourself in the third person.
For example, do not say "Joe Jones has had 20 years of experience." Everyone knows that you, Joe Jones, are the person paying for the ad, unless a hospital or other establishment has taken out the ad.

Rule #2: Brag—it's okay!

I know it can feel a little awkward at first, but your clients *want* you to have confidence. People want have total trust in their practitioner, and they won't if you don't have confidence in yourself. They want to know that you have received the right training, that you are not going to injure or humiliate them, and that they are going to feel absolutely wonderful by the time they walk out of your office. If you don't believe this about yourself and state it with conviction, who will?

List your certifications and degrees, and spell out anything that is not immediately obvious to your readers. Most people are familiar with the initials "M.D." to indicate a medical doctor, but are you sure they know what an "N.D." (Doctor of Naturopathy) is? Also list your areas of specialty such as shiatsu or deep muscle massage, couples counseling, ear candling—whatever. If you prefer to do only one kind of massage, or one form of psychotherapy, go into a little more detail about your process. If you do several kinds of massage or psychotherapy, it's okay to list them all. Each one of these approaches has an advantage.

The one thing you want to avoid is stretching the truth to the point where the expectations of the client are much greater than what you can actually deliver. Therefore, if you list a number of offerings, try to set one of them up as your primary area of expertise. Otherwise, you can come across on paper as being spread too thin to cover anything well. And never, ever lie.

Rule #3: Get right to the point.

Don't waste a lot of verbiage in the beginning of the ad. Try to be concise and state things clearly. Forego the use of jargon and anything sounding too new age-y. In the early days, alternative therapies were largely relegated to fringe populations, but today they've become mainstream, and even upscale in some instances. Jargon will narrow your audience; you want to expand it.

Rule #4: Word your ideas in a positive way.

You don't want to use terminology that connotes negatives like can't, won't, shouldn't, etc. For example, instead of saying, "We can't take all insurances." You might want to say, "Insurances accepted from New England Health and Harvard Pilgrim," or whatever your companies are. Play with ways to put your ideas into a positive framework.

Make it simple and inviting. Think of an ad as an appetizer—easy to consume, not overwhelming. The main course will be discovered when the client gets to your office. Don't get too technical. Try to break anything that is too long into smaller pieces. Use bullets if necessary.

Time to Get It Down on Paper

Okay, now it's time to write. Just write down what you think would constitute an acceptable ad. Let your thoughts flow. One way to judge whether or not you like your ad, is to read it out loud to yourself. Inevitably, you will hear something that is not quite right, or does not really sound like you. Once you've adjusted for that, look at your sentence structure. Is there anything convoluted or wordy that could be made more clear?

If you are not sure of your grammar and punctuation, consult someone with advanced editing skills—perhaps a teacher. Even though your clients are coming to you for a massage and not a creative writing class, they want to be assured of your total professionalism, and this is one more area that can either make you look good or not-so-good. I know this all too well from having made typos in my client's ads that make them look sloppy, or worse, unintelligent. Even if you are not a grammarian yourself, your clients will know that you've enlisted the help of someone who is, because after all, you are a professional businessperson, and that's what professional people do. If they don't have the answers, they hire people who do.

Look back over the text you've written for your ad. Check to make sure you have included your name (or the name of your business) and your office address. If you work from home, you might not want to put your home address in an ad. Instead, you can indicate the town in which you live, and wait until a client calls you before divulging your address.

You also must have a way for people to reach you, so include a phone number and/or an email address. Now look at the way you have described your business. Is there a way to pare this down so that if it appeared in a display ad in the newspaper, you would have enough white space? Here is where the use of bullets comes in handy. Rather than spelling out your areas of expertise in paragraph form, list them as bulleted items. They are easier on the eyes and faster to consume than wading through whole paragraphs.

Visuals

Once you are satisfied with the text, you are ready to begin creating the rest of the ad. How do you want to present yourself visually? Do you consider yourself traditional or contemporary? Playful? Serious? A maverick? Again, a graphic artist can produce the final version of your ad, but you need to think about what your visual presentation will say about you.

The font you choose can tell someone a great deal as well. Some fonts are very blocky-looking and suggest weight, masculinity, sturdiness, etc. Other lighter fonts and scripted fonts are considered more feminine, playful, and whimsical. There are literally hundreds of fonts in between. See Figure 8-1 for some of the most common fonts. Each one appears in the actual name of the font. Look down the list of fonts and see which ones attract you. All of these fonts appear in the same point size.

Are you going to use a photo of yourself? It is usually a good idea provided the photo is a good one. Every bit of information you can give to clients before they arrive at your door is a plus for you. Many people feel more comfortable going to someone whose face they have already seen. Don't use just any old photo because, if it is of poor quality or does not have the appropriate contrast, it can do more harm than good. Also, don't use a photo that is more than two or three years old. I know a woman who has been using the same photo for at least 15 years, and this is truly false advertising.

Most newspapers and magazines can work with black and white or color photos. Your primary concern should be whether or not your face is well lit and clear. Surprisingly, sometimes a simple pass-

Figure 6-1.
An assortment of type fonts.

Fabulous Fonts

Americana	**Eras Demi**
Arial	**Formal Script**
Arnold Boecklin	Freehand Script
Avant Garde	Futura Light
Baskerville	Goudy Handtooled
Benguiat	**Hobo**
BERMUDA	Juice
Bernhard Fashion	*Lucinda Calligraphy*
Blackmoor	Mister Television
Blippo Black	Mistral
Bookman Oldstyle	O C R
Broadway	Optima
Brush Script	New Century Schoolbook
Comic Sans	Park Avenue
Cooper Black	Pink Flamingo
COPPERPLATE	**STENCIL**
CREEPY	Times New Roman
Curlz	uncial
Delphin	*Viner Hand*
Edwardian Script	Wendy

---

port picture works better than anything else. They are specifically set-up to show the features of your face with clarity, and they are probably the least expensive way of presenting yourself through a photograph.

Do you have a graphic? A simple graphic design can be very pleasing, and is a sure way to distinguish you from other therapists visually. Don't use Chinese or Japanese calligraphy unless it's unique to your profession, because you may find that other people are using the exact same thing. Whatever graphic you use should be very easy to decipher. Don't use something so intricate that you have to practically turn it upside in order to figure out what it says or means.

Earlier I referred to the need for white space in a display ad. The idea behind white space is that your eye is drawn immediately to the text; if there is too much copy, especially if it involves too many type sizes or fonts, the ad will appear to be cluttered. Look through newspapers and magazines, and without actually reading the text, see which ones attract your eyes the fastest. Often people make the mistake of thinking that they have to cram as much information as possible into an ad in order get their money's worth. The truth is, simplicity is best. Along these lines, you never want your ad copy to run all the way to the edge of the margins.

Once you have the copy and the graphics figured out, you'll need to establish a budget, and choose the vehicles for your advertising. You'll need business cards to hand to people everywhere you go, brochures that explain in further depth what kind of services you offer, and you'll need that very important newspaper or magazine ad. You don't necessarily need your own stationery or envelopes, especially at first when money is an issue. Eventually, these latter two items will round out your professional presentation to the public, but you can get by without them for now.

My recommendation is that, at least in the beginning, you advertise in as many places as your budget can afford. We're going to be going over the pros and cons of a number of different advertising vehicles, but first there are a couple of things I want to say about advertising in general.

Advertising Tips

Ideally, as you begin to advertise and bring in clients, the places where you advertise will indicate whether or not your money is best spent there by the sheer number of responses you receive. Equipped with this information, you can begin to concentrate on the ad vehicles that are really paying off. Eventually, you may find that word-of-mouth recommendations alone will keep you in business, but even then, you may want to continue to advertise in a small number of places. Why? Because advertising keeps your name in front of the public, it underscores the legitimacy of your business, and secures your place in the business community. It may also fill the occasional empty slot in your practice. Before you can rely on word-of-mouth, you need to see a large number of clients. In order to see a large number of clients, you have to have your strategy all mapped out.

As we go along, keep in mind, that although you have your basic notion of what you want to say in your ads, you may need to tweak the copy a little to suit the ad vehicle you choose. In other words, ad copy for a radio ad will most likely be somewhat different than the copy for a print ad.

Also, it is important to keep your advertising up-to-date. If you've just started using heated stones in your massage therapy practice, be sure that all your advertising now includes that wording. If your email address or your phone number changes, be sure to contact all the places where your ad appears to make updates. It's a very good idea to have an advertising calendar so that you can check the deadlines for the newspapers and magazines to which you send your ads. Do not rely on them to contact you. This is an important part of your business operation, because if you miss the deadline for your favorite holistic health magazine, it may be another three months before your name is out there again.

What should you expect from advertising? This is a tough one. Experts will tell you that the public needs to see your name nine times before they will actually pick up the phone and call you. I think nine is a pessimistic number, but the truth is that you may not get a response to your ad immediately, no matter how good it is. I know this from my own experience in responding to ads.

Before I bought *Many Hands Magazine* from Beyond Words Bookshop, I used to pick it up and go through the ads myself. One of them caught my eye in the psychic section. I was at a crossroads in my life and was curious, but hesitant, about getting a reading. I didn't call right away. In fact I didn't call until the fourth issue that featured this person's ad—almost a whole year later. It is frequently the case that we just need a little time to think about whatever service is offered before we actually take advantage of it, especially if the service is new to us. Many holistic practices, such as massage therapy, psychotherapy, and psychic readings, are highly personal, making it necessary for a little lead-time for people to warm up to the idea of using the service.

Then there is the other extreme where an ad gets great responses right off the bat because your ad hit the clients at the right time with the right information, and they were ready to act. So, there are people who will never respond no matter how great the ad, and people who respond immediately, but the largest group by far is the curious public who edges toward the phone, taking weeks or months to get there. Therefore, patience is required, which can be very hard to exercise. Sometimes, it can feel like you're watching those precious advertising dollars disappear into a black hole. I used to feel somewhat hesitant talking new people into advertising because the truth is, I could never guarantee the result. I could only advise clients on the design and text of their ads, and do the best I could to make sure the ad came out correctly and on time, or I would have to refund some of the money. Don't be fooled by an ad rep who claims to guarantee you results, because it is virtually impossible to do that. No one can know who will answer your ad, or how many calls you will get.

What's important to remember is that you don't want to put an ad in the paper, or anywhere else, until you are really ready. That means covering all the things we've discussed so far *plus* being mentally prepared. Many of my newer clients would call two weeks before the deadline for ad rates. I made a note of them, and if I hadn't heard anything from them closer to the deadline, I would call them back. Sometimes, they would decide to jump in—the deadline seemed to be the push they needed, but others would shy away stating they were not ready. For many newcomers, it's like jumping into a cold pool of water, and hoping their body will adjust to the temperature quickly.

Some potential advertisers would drag their feet and say they just didn't have *time* to write an ad right then. I could tell from their voices that they would really like to be able to pull this off, but they just couldn't. Most likely they were having trouble getting other aspects of their business into smooth running order as well. Hesitation of this kind is an important signal that there is a distraction from the work. If this applies to you, don't worry. Take your time. Run through your checklists again. Ask a friend or two to play "client" and run through a practice session with them several times. Practice answering your phone, and discussing your various policies. These actions will build your confidence.

When You're Ready

Let's say you've taken the plunge. We will go over lots of advertising choices and what you can expect from ad reps, but for now let's look at another aspect of advertising: continuing to advertise when the clients aren't calling. Every one of your dollars counts, so why would you hang in there with a newspaper or magazine that isn't producing any results. The answer is that they are *always* producing a result (name recognition), just not an actual client walking through your door. In other words, let's say you take out an ad in a magazine that prints quarterly, and you've given it three issues and nothing has happened. You might have received one or two calls, but they didn't result in a client. By the way, why not? Every call you get is a person who saw your ad and liked it. If they call you and don't come in for a massage, the gap in the process may be your conversation with them. Was it the price? Was it your tone? Did you sound like an amateur?

The reason you want to hang in there with ads that don't produce clients right away, is because you are building name recognition. Remember that the public may need to see your name several times before taking action. If you are very sure that the newspaper or magazine you are advertising in is an ethical, high quality paper, and you know that the audience reading it is the audience you want to reach, then even if they don't call, it may be well worth it to continue. No one knows that you are not getting clients from the ad but you. On the other hand, everyone who is reading the magazine is seeing that you are out there, including your fellow massage therapists with whom you might want to network at some point. When your name is mentioned, someone will say, "Oh, yes, I saw him in the paper," or "I've heard of him." When I had casual conversations about my magazine, inevitably someone would say, "Oh, I've seen her ad, and I've been meaning to call her. I just haven't gotten around to it yet."

You just never know when this kind of patience will pay off. I've seen it happen over and over again. An advertiser will call to say they have had no response after three issues and they want to bail. Two weeks later, right before the deadline, they call to get back into the next issue because they finally got some clients from the ad. Furthermore, even though many practitioners receive their clients by word-of-mouth, they will continue to advertise to fill those three or four empty spots in their schedule, so as to ensure a steady stream of clients throughout the week or month.

And here's an interesting little tidbit. People asked me all the time why some ads pull and others don't. Provided that all other things are equal and satisfactory—text, visuals, etc.—the only common thread I've noticed is bill payment practices. The people who pay their bills on time, are the people who are also getting the responses they wanted. At first this didn't make any sense to me because of course the general public doesn't have a clue as to whether the advertiser pays his or her bills on time. It seemed on the surface to be karmic payback.

But the more I thought about it, the more I realized that the people who pay on time are the ones who are organized. When you are organized, you are confident, when you are confident, you are ready for clients, when you are ready for clients, they will show up. And to take the whole thing full circle, when an invoice comes to you, the practitioner, *you* are ready to pay it on time because you have planned ahead. You have planned ahead because you are organized!

These are the people who have thought about their businesses. They have created their ads on time because they are enthusiastic about what they do. When someone is enthusiastic, it's not hard for that person to come up with the words to describe what he or she does and has to offer. Because they have taken care of all the little details beforehand, they are free to give their energy to their clients. This comes through in their voices on the phone, and their demeanor during a session.

Interestingly, being well prepared and organized go hand in hand with the revolving door theory. When you push on one side of a revolving door, the other side opens. The same is true for your business. Something gets set in motion when you take your first step and you are really ready to do it. You begin to move a certain energy forward and as you gain momentum, you draw in a wider and wider circle of people with the same energy around you.

Summary

Take time with your software and play with the various functions until you're comfortable using it. Use the exercises described here to figure out who you are in business, how you want to present yourself, and create some written copy for the purpose of advertising. Wait until you're truly ready to present yourself to the world, and then choose the right advertising vehicle(s) for your practice.

CHAPTER NINE

Advertising Media

This chapter contains quite a bit of information about advertising which can be a lifeline to the world for your new business. You may have a small budget and may only be able to advertise very minimally right now, but I encourage you to read about the variety of ways to advertise your services, because some of them may surprise you in terms of cost and effectiveness. I've seen ads for holistic practices in virtually every form of advertising mentioned here, so nothing should be ruled out. You may get ideas you wouldn't have thought of before, and it is always good to know what your competition is doing in terms of advertising. The more information you have, the better position you're in to make decisions regarding your business.

What Should You Expect?

What should you be looking for from editors, ad reps, and station managers? What service should you expect from the magazine or newspaper (both are referred to generally as "papers") you are advertising in, or the radio or TV station that's running your spot? This varies from rep to rep, and from ad vehicle to ad vehicle.

Some magazines will put your ad together for you for free. Others will charge you by the hour for design, and still others may include an additional initial set-up fee. Most papers today expect that an ad will come to them all ready to be printed. Either it reaches them by email in a specific format (we'll discuss format later) or it will reach them by mail in camera-ready form.

Some of the smaller papers will do the work for you as long as you provide them with a thumbnail sketch of how you want the ad to look, and a typewritten version of your text. They are willing to do this because the way your ad looks in their paper has a huge impact on whether or not other people will want to advertise with them. Therefore they prefer to size it in an aesthetically pleasing and professional-looking manner.

If the paper is designing the ad for you, insist on receiving a proof of the ad before the paper goes to press. Check it carefully and call the paper immediately if you find an error. Do not expect the paper to chase you down if you decide to leave town for a few days. In case you need to make changes to the ad, you should know that newspapers will not hold up their production schedule for you, so pay close attention to the time by which you need to get any changes back to them.

Remember that savvy media sales people are very good at figuring out how to spend your hard-earned advertising budget. Don't be intimidated. Trust your own instincts, and stay in control of your finances; don't cave in to ad costs you can't afford. Newspapers and magazines need and want your money, but if their charges seem too expensive, try to negotiate the price, or look for another option.

Terminology

Each form of advertising uses a different terminology for the way ads are sold. Advertising in newspapers, magazines, and Yellow Pages are sold according to space. Newspapers and magazines in particular usually go by the "column inch." This refers to the depth an ad takes up in one column of the newspaper.

Radio ads are sold in 30-second or 60-second units, which can be organized into what's called a 13-week "flight," or series of ads that run at the same time each week. Your 30-second spot running for 13 weeks in a row can be very effective. TV stations refer to ads as "spots."

Other terms refer to the computerized format you use to email your ad. For example, let's say you've created an ad in Photoshop, Publisher or Microsoft Word and you want to email it to your local paper. There are several ways you can send it depending on what it is going to be used for. You don't need to remember these formats right at this moment—it can be daunting going through all this information, but the terms are jpeg, eps, gif, tiff, and pdf. The important thing to remember is that computers and software differ widely. You need to be sure you know what the newspaper's requirements are, and that your ad is created in a compatible format for that newspaper.

There are also several different types of ads. First, there is display advertising. When you purchase a display ad, you are buying a finite amount of space, for example a five-inch ad. This would be an ad five inches high and one column width across—very vertical. A five by three ad would be five inches high and three column widths across—a totally different shape than the first.

Second are classified ads that involve a price per word or per line, are usually small, appear in the back of the newspaper or magazine, and are used for announcing things like office space that is available for rent. A small classified ad can be quite effective for some types of practices.

Third are directory listings, which vary from magazine to magazine, but in the holistic community, they usually are very cost effective, offering a favorable amount of space to describe your craft without a huge price tag. Typically, they appear in the second half of a magazine and run horizontally across the page. They often feature a photograph and/or a graphic, followed by a paragraph description of the practitioner and his or her business.

Another aspect of advertising media is the price structure and its availability to you. Newspapers and magazines are usually straightforward with their pricing; it's possible to obtain their rates in writing by asking for their rate sheet or rate card. In my experience, it's been difficult get rates as easily from the Yellow Pages, radio or TV. The latter seem to allow their sales reps a lot of latitude when it comes to pricing, so be prepared to negotiate. The figures I list here are approximations and will almost certainly vary with different regions of the country.

Beginning

Holistic businesses today are faced with tough challenges. Costs are increasing, competition within the marketplace is tightening, and vendors seem to be providing less and less support. In addition, customers have grown more cautious about how and where they spend their money. Before you place an ad for your business you need to have answers to relevant questions such as: *Do people read the newspaper anymore? Which of your customers watch television? Is cable a wise investment? Are the Yellow Pages an effective use of your ad dollars? Will anyone see your outdoor ad and act on it? Will people respond to your direct mail campaign?*

Not to worry. This section is designed to help you understand and evaluate the basic strengths of each medium, and will also explore the concerns many advertisers share about each one. The best decisions are informed decisions, and the material presented in these pages will help you make intelligent choices on which medium, or combination of media, offers the best solution to your sales and marketing problems.

Business Cards, Brochures, and Flyers

Business cards are usually a standard size, but can be printed in either a vertical or horizontal format. The more expensive cards will be constructed of a heavier paper stock and can even be made in leather or vinyl. They can be printed in one color, usually black type on a white card, two-color such as black and red type on a white card, or four-color which actually includes all colors. Four-color refers to the use of cyan, magenta, yellow and black (CMYK) printing plates that are used in layers to create virtually every color of the rainbow. Naturally, four-color printing is the most expensive.

Because of their small size, the information contained on a business card should be short and sweet. It should include your name and/or business name, your business address, your phone number, and your email address. If the name of your business does not make it obvious as to what you do, then a single line of text should be added to cover that. More type than that can be too much reading material, particularly if your text must also accommodate a graphic.

I like to see the name of the person I'm dealing with. I find it hard to relate to a business name like "Soothing Surroundings" with only an email address as contact information. Some businesses may be able to get away with a business name and an email address these days, but the holistic community is best served by a more personal means of contact, like a name and a phone number.

Business cards can be used in a variety of creative ways. For example, you can attach several of your cards to the bottom of the flyer you're placing on a community bulletin board with glue drops that come on a sheet. These sheets can be purchased in most drug and craft stores. They can be easily removed by a potential client who will now have more of your necessary information, instead of just your name and phone number.

You want to get in the habit of taking your business cards on the road with you everywhere you go. Whenever you find a doctor's office, grocery store, natural food store, or college kiosk that will allow you to leave your business card and/or brochure, go for it. Keep some in your car just in case. Hand one to the mailman, the person standing in line behind you, the other people pumping gas into their cars, etc. This is a good practice, especially if you are a little shy. Every time you approach a stranger, it helps to break that shyness down. Simply explain to people that you are opening a new practice in town and you'd like them to keep you in mind if they ever need a massage. Some people will take the card and walk away, or, walk away without taking the card, but lots of people will engage in a conversation. You can use this opportunity to toot your horn, explain what you do, and why your practice is unique.

Brochures are an expansion of your verbal presentation and your written advertisement. They offer you the chance to describe your practice in detail. Like the business card and any other advertising vehicle, you'll need your name and/or business name, business address, phone number, and email address. First you want to describe what you do. Use bullets for your various services if you offer more than one. You may also want to include some historical information about your craft, what results a client can expect, what products you might sell, and other special benefits like heated stone therapy, facials in addition to massage, etc. Ask clients for quotes regarding your skills to use in your brochure. When someone seems to be making vast improvements because of your particular technique, ask them what they would say about your work, and if it would be permissible to quote them. Most people will be flattered that you asked.

Brochures typically have six panels: one on the front, two panels on the back, and three panels in the interior. Take an 8.5-inch by 11-inch piece of paper and fold it into thirds to see what this would look like. The front panel should be very similar to your business card in terms of what you include on it. Retain the same font and graphic(s) to create instant recognition by using the same visual elements for all your printed materials.

The interior of the brochure is generally reserved for a full description of your work—maybe the history on one panel, another panel for paragraph descriptions of your techniques, and another panel for bulleted items. Here again, you do not want to overwhelm clients with too much information or too much visual clutter.

Now flip to the back panel. You can use one panel for quotes from your clients, and on the panel that will be showing once the brochure is fully folded, you can design a coupon, or include a photograph or line drawing of your office, or a map showing where your office is located. Use your imagination. Follow the basic rules and you can't go wrong.

Yellow Pages

The first edition of the Yellow Pages appeared in the late 1800's when the Wyoming Telephone Company allegedly ran out of white paper and started printing on yellow. Since that time, the Yellow Pages have proliferated to the point where there are now many different versions, including several for the same metropolitan area. According to Competitive Media Facts, the Yellow Pages won in a survey of people who were asked where they turn first to find a business in their community.

Some communities will list a business for free, or at a very minimal cost, with a single line listing that includes your business name and phone number. The Yellow Pages reinforce your presence in the community where you live. Of course your listing there is not an indication of how skillful or ethical you are; it simply adds some reassurance to inquiring customers as to the existence of your business.

Advertising in the Yellow Pages is also advantageous because almost every household in the country has one version or another. People who are using them have already determined that they want your product or service, so there is no need to "sell" your product or service in the traditional sense. Initially, the Yellow Pages were printed with black ink only, but over time production has become more sophisticated; today it's possible to purchase four-color display ads.

A negative aspect of the Yellow Pages is that the reps are trained to encourage advertisers to take out a large space, and place an actual ad, instead of just placing a line listing. How are Yellow Pages sold? You decide how much money you want to spend and the representative will help you determine the size and placement of the ad, but it may be difficult to get an exact price from the sales people unless you are willing to actually meet with them in person.

Other disadvantages include the distraction of ads other than yours on the page, and competition from electronic Yellow Pages, which are capable of updating information virtually instantaneously. Since Yellow Pages are only published once a year, the information will remain the same even if you moved and changed your number eight months ago.

Daily Newspapers

As I mentioned earlier, advertisements in newspapers are sold by the column inch. You can get a variety of rates from a daily paper that will include daily rates, weekly rates, monthly rates, and yearly rates. Sometimes papers will have a special health section one day a week, or they may have their own quarterly health magazine, which is also a great place to advertise.

According to some sources, newspapers lost nearly five million readers over the last ten years for two reasons: there are fewer subscribers (people do not read the paper as much as they used to), and because there are so many other sources of information available.

The under 30 crowd, for example, gets much of its information from the Internet, YouTube, and online versions of major newspapers such as the New York Times. Newspapers have been forced to add their own online versions in order to compete. As paper costs continue to rise, the cost of advertising must necessarily go up for newspapers to retain their profit margin.

An additional disadvantage to advertising in newspapers is that, like the Yellow Pages, there can be many other ads crammed onto a page competing for the eye of the reader. Your ad may not be noticed if the placement is poor.

In a typical daily newspaper about two-thirds of the content consists of advertising. The Sunday edition might contain more, not counting inserts and circulars. The cost of a newspaper ad will vary with the region in which you are advertising, but generally may range from $25 per column inch in small towns to over $1,000 per column inch in major metropolitan areas. Most papers have a two-inch minimum. Another factor affecting the cost is where the ad appears in the paper (main, business, sports section, etc.), which day it appears (Sundays are more expensive), and how frequently you run it. One plus for newspapers is that they enjoy a great deal of loyalty and most of the actual *subscribers* read the paper every day.

Magazines

There are many different kinds of magazines from the slick, glossy magazines you find in drug stores, newsrooms, and bookstores to the free newsprint versions that have grown so wildly in the last ten years, often featuring alternative health and political slants for local and regional areas. Magazines may sell ads by the column inch or they may simply state rates for certain sizes. A business card size might be $100, or a 4" by 4" ad might sell for $215. Usually the smaller the ad, the more expensive it is relative to size. In other words, a $100 ad is only one eighth of a typical 8.5 inch by 11-inch page, while a full page goes for $500—not $800. This rate structure allows magazines to entice people to invest in larger ads.

Magazines may be published monthly, bi-monthly or quarterly. Usually, the longer the time lag between publishing dates, the meatier the editorial section. People are inclined to hang onto a magazine with a large number of articles, which they often pass around the office or home. The disadvantage to a quarterly magazine, however, is that you have to wait three months before your ad will be seen again.

On the other hand, monthly magazines may not have much content and are usually put together in a hurry. No matter what kind of magazine you choose, make sure it is of a high enough quality for your ad. Look it over carefully and decide whether or not you want to be associated with the other advertisers in the magazine. Yes, you can save money by going with a cheaper magazine, but in the end it may do you no good.

Every year hundreds of new magazines appear, but, like newspapers, magazines are read less frequently than they used to be. Reaching the coveted under 30 market by advertising in magazines is harder to do since this cohort of the market is turning to the Internet for information about products and services. Also, magazines can suffer from ad clutter making it hard for your ad to stand out. As far as free magazines go, many stores and businesses that once welcomed these quarterly or bi-monthly publications, will not take them anymore because there are simply too many of them out there.

Magazines that specialize in particular subjects offer advertisers a chance to connect with a targeted market. Look for a magazine that zeros in on that audience, check out the quality, and ask how many readers are included in the circulation. Will it reach everyone you hope to reach, or is the target area too small to be effective? Keep in mind that, as I mentioned earlier, magazines are often passed around, left on buses and trains, available in the naturopath's or chiropractor's waiting room, etc. Therefore, your ad is likely to be seen by three times the number cited as the actual circulation.

So, what does this all add up to? By advertising in a magazine you can reach a certain audience, and your ad will have the advantage of visual appeal. Doing research on the magazine's circulation, target market, and printing schedule will make it easier for you to choose wisely.

Magazine ad rates vary according to the quality and frequency of production, and are usually described in terms of the amount of space they take up on a page: $^1/_4$, $^1/_3$, $^1/_2$, $^2/_3$, $^3/_4$, and a full page. Display ads in the free newsprint variety can range from $100 to $2,000; while ads in the glossier versions are much more expensive running from $10,000 to $35,000. Back covers in both types of magazines are usually the most expensive placements.

Broadcast TV

The first appearance of the CRT (Cathode Ray Tube) occurred in 1936 so TV, as we're come to know it, has been around for over 70 years. In that time, it has undergone numerous changes; today there are many other viewing choices including pay-per-view, DVDs, VCRs, TiVo, Netflix, the Internet, iPhones and so on.

Digital television, or DTV, will soon be another option. DTV is on a government-mandated track to replace the current analog system by 2009. As the deadline approaches, High Definition Television (a subset of DTV) signals are being broadcast in dozens of markets.

In broadcast TV, a 30-second spot is the industry standard for one ad. The cost can be negotiated, especially during slack times of the year. Ask for the station's cost per thousand (CPM). This is what it's going to cost you to reach all the members of your target audience. Many stations want you to run an ad for three months, which can cost several thousand dollars. It is very hard to isolate an actual figure unless you are in serious negotiations with the station, but most likely the costs are high.

Remember that TV and radio sales people are going to try to sell you their product. They usually don't have standardized rates available on paper, but instead will ask you how much you want to spend, what audience you want to reach, etc. Talking to several different reps to do some comparison-shopping can take a lot of time.

When obtaining information about costs, ask if you will be charged for the production of your commercial. Broadcast TV prices for production range from $200 to $1,500 and up. Sometimes there are additional fees for advertising agency commissions and production companies. For example, if an ad agency created your TV ad, and negotiated with station RUOK to run it, the ad agency wants a 10% cut of the cost from you.

The advantage to purchasing a TV spot is the widespread use of TV. The majority of viewers spend as much as seven hours a day watching, and most have grown up with TV. One single exposure can reach millions of people. Unlike print media, TV has the attraction of sound and motion to grab attention.

On the other hand, according to some sources, television's network prime time audience has decreased dramatically because of all the other viewing options mentioned above. To avoid commercials, other promotions, and public service announcements (PSAs), which now amount to 25% of each prime-time hour, people will flip through channels quickly, or change to programs that have no ads like the independent movie channels.

Cable TV

Cable TV provided an alternative to broadcast TV three decades ago, but disappointed its initial fans with its relatively primitive technology and programming quality until fairly recently. Today there have been upgrades to the physical plants that house cable TV stations, an expansion of interconnected markets, and improved software, making cable more appealing to advertisers, according to industry sources.

The cost of a cable ad is referred to as "underwriting" because your dollars are supporting the station. Cable TV ads are dirt cheap by comparison with broadcast TV and the audience is large; over half of all American homes have cable TV. Prime time broadcast spots can cost $2,000-$3,000 versus $175. The stations reserve four to six spots per hour for local ads. Thanks to digital technology, you can insert your ad when you want it to show, but this is done on a first come, first served basis so you must act early in the process.

Improvements in the cable industry have made production of cable ads more professional looking, employing all the plusses of TV advertising such as motion, sound, and visual appeal. Cable's ratings typically increase during the summer, when regular television ratings decline due to reruns.

Radio

The Radio Advertising Bureau claims that radio may be a good choice as an advertising medium since it offers "superior targetability, listener loyalty, ad recall, and message retention." People tend to listen to one or two of their favorite stations on a regular basis as they drive to and from work in the car, or with headphones on while mowing the lawn. As with magazines, you can target the audience you want in order to draw in the kind of clients you want. People in the radio industry refer to "image transfer," which means you hear the radio commercial and then you picture the product that you've seen in other media. This reinforces awareness of the product or service.

The 1996 Telecommunications Act allowed radio stations to compete with other media like newspapers and magazines by joining forces, but now radio faces competition from podcasts made available through iPods and the Internet. A potential disadvantage to a radio ad, is that if your ad is only played once a day at the same time, only a small portion of the listening audience will hear it. Moreover, when a commercial comes on, many listeners turn to other channels.

A typical thirty-second national radio spot can cost hundreds of dollars. Like representatives from the Yellow Pages and TV, radio reps may not be inclined to give you an exact figure for your advertising over the phone. Many station reps recommend a 13-week flight of 30-second spots to develop product awareness.

Outdoor Advertising

According to the Welcoming Ministry of the United Methodist Church, "outdoor advertising—particularly the billboard—remains the champion of the generic and all-inclusive. Far from a tightly targeted medium, billboards are positioned as a way to reach large, undifferentiated audiences." The Outdoor Advertising Association of America reports that billboards are doing well.

Competitive Media Facts claims many people think only of billboards when thinking of outdoor advertising, but there are lots of other ways to advertise outdoors including fast food chains, car dealerships, amusement parks, signage on transit and bus shelters, on bus exteriors, sandwich signs on sidewalks, and street furniture such as public benches.

Billboard technology today employs vinyl photographs, three-dimensional effects, backlighting, digital and LED technology, computerized lighting, and even giant flat screen TV effects. And, as we've all seen at highway repair sites, or on buildings outside New York and other cities, electronic signs can allow several messages to flash sequentially on one sign alone.

Nonetheless, outdoor advertising has its disadvantages. A billboard has to communicate its message immediately, making it necessary for limiting the number of words that appear and making it mandatory that the visual image can be understand instantaneously.

The cost of a single billboard can be staggering at between $3,500 and $7,000, but the cost per thousand is relatively low because so many people will see it. The cost of other outdoor advertising varies with whatever vehicle you choose. If you decide to go this route, think carefully about how you would associate the image of your business on the side of a bus, for example. Outdoor advertising can be effective for communicating short messages and simple ideas or concepts in high traffic areas. It is not affected by seasonal changes in the way TV can be, but it is subject to municipal codes and environmental regulations.

The effectiveness of outdoor advertising is virtually impossible to determine. Once your billboard has been erected, it will stay up for the duration of your contract. A typical ad must be purchased 28 days prior to its showing to allow time for production and placement, which prohibits any corrections or additions that may result from changing business conditions.

Now there is an entirely new wrinkle in the outdoor ad biz: spinning. An advertiser can hire a company that will design a sign extolling the virtues of their practice, and that company employs someone to go out on the street and literally spin the sign. The sign spinning performance is dramatic enough to stop traffic. Imagine a street performer, throwing a sign in the air the way a pizza maker throws dough, and spinning around while he does so. It's an interesting idea, but probably too expensive for you, and so far it's only available in Los Angeles, Chicago, and New York City.

Internet, Web Banners, and Email

The Internet has grown by leaps and bounds in the last decade with advertising revenues reaching the one billion dollar mark in 2008 for "behavioral advertising," according to the Internet Advertising Bureau (IAB). Behavioral advertising specifically targets online customers based on their activities via the Internet.

Internet ads are sold in the forms of banners and pop-ups for a certain amount of time, or what are called "impressions." Impressions refer to how many times the banner is drawn to the screen, as opposed to how many times the banner is clicked on. Therefore, the price is dependent on how many people access the page, and thus see the banner ad. Sometimes there is an additional charge for a link. Be very certain that your ad appears on a reputable site that is not subject to legal proceedings against them for copyright infringement, etc. You could be linked with that site—electronically and legally.

If you have a website, its desirable to be one of the first listings to appear on a search engine since most people will access the first couple sites that appear. With pay per click advertising, you pay for the ad only when someone clicks on your ad in order to get further information. At 1¢ per click, this can be an inexpensive and cost effective way to advertise, although some of the more popular sites can charge as much as 50¢ or more. A "click through" refers to the number of times a user actually clicks on your ad relative to the number of times the ad appeared (number of impressions).

The advantage of the Internet is that it is a very direct form of advertising, one that allows clients to make purchases with the simple click of a mouse. It also gives an advertiser the capability of actually "conversing" directly with clients in real time online, so that you can find out what your clients like and what they don't. Internet technology allows you to measure exactly how many people saw your message by counting hits to the site where your message appears, and you can change your message instantly so the information stays current.

The disadvantages of the internet are computer breakdowns and downtime; users getting sick of seeing pop-up ads and blocking them out, slow downloading time for pages filled with graphics, and online security issues. Online credit card fraud is a scary and growing phenomenon. If you are selling holistic products online, you will need to assure your clientele that ordering online is safe, and that your site is secure.

Email can be an effective way of reaching your clients for special promotions. Create several different types of emails before you open your business, so that you have a number of "boilerplate" specials. Use your logo or other identifying graphics and fonts, and set them up so that all you have to do is change the dates now and then. Add your clients to your address book as a group so that you can do mass emailings when you want to reach them all.

Direct Mail

Many advertisers love direct mail because of its ability to reach so many homes directly, but many consumers hate it for the same reason, according to the Hampton Roads Small Business Development Center.

Direct mail is a great way to stay in touch with your clients. I used direct mail as my primary means of announcing specials, promotions, and broadcasting the next deadline for my magazine. Every time I got a new lead, I added that person to my mailing list—even if they never advertised with me. Sometimes people received mailings from me for several years before they actually sent in an ad. I obtained leads from lots of different sources: people who called me, business cards posted on bulletin boards, sidewalk sandwich signs, the Internet, and many others. Some of the people on my list advertised years ago and dropped out. I kept them on my list because in many cases—enough cases to make it worthwhile—they would come back and advertise again. To keep costs down, however, I did scan the list periodically and take out people I was certain I would never hear from again.

The least expensive way I've found, that also gives me enough space to say what I need to say, is to mail a single sheet—a double-sided flyer, folded in thirds, with the address showing. It's very inexpensive to have the flyers printed—500 for $30—and you can go to a UPS store to have them stamped and sealed. Sealing is essential because the post office will not allow unsealed mail to go through the system. If you have any questions about what you can mail, talk to the post office before you order your direct mail pieces.

Also, I always use first class mail because it's faster and better handled. You can save yourself the cost of sealing and stamping by doing it yourself while watching TV. In every direct mailing I sent out, I included one mailed to my home and one to my office so I could make sure that they all went out as planned and on time.

Direct mail can target consumers by a wide variety of categories available on database information systems such as their age, location, products they've purchased in the past, and special interests. It can reach a large number of people, especially if you have a direct mail insert in your local paper. Direct mail that goes directly to your customer base, helps to build a relationship with your clientele by keeping them informed about your operations, any new equipment you may be using, specials you're offering, etc. It is also easy to track direct mail responses.

Unfortunately the disadvantages also have to do with response rate. Most direct mail marketers consider a response rate of only two or three percent to be successful, meaning that the rest of the recipients will toss your mailer into the trash, thus the term "junk mail."

Even among consumers who are not actively trying to have their names stricken from direct mailing lists, there are many who move each year, making it difficult for direct mail companies to identify and maintain accurate databases. Like everything else, direct mail costs are on the rise. Increases in postal rates and paper costs are disadvantages to this form of advertising.

If you have a special going, you can buy pre-paid postcards and have your special information printed on the cards—that way you don't have to go through the stamping process. Also you can print self-stick labels and apply them yourself, or go to a mailing service that will do that for you. Anytime you go to a mailing house you are adding to the cost per item by about 3-7 cents depending on whether they are also doing the sealing for a larger piece.

Alternative Newsweeklies

The alternative newsweekly offers a slant slightly off the center of traditional news reporting. As these small papers proliferated across the country, they developed loyal followings among younger readers, often educated and affluent, who didn't relate to the more traditional presentation of the news through daily newspapers. Since that time, many of these smaller weeklies have been purchased as adjuncts to the larger daily conglomerates, providing an additional source of income.

Newsweeklies are usually distributed on racks, store shelves or floors, library entrances, and the front porches or hallways of office buildings, throughout a specific region. Most are available free of charge, and like magazines, are carried everywhere.

An ad in a newsweekly offers many of the same characteristics as a newspaper ad, but at lower rates. Unfortunately, many of these papers look cheaply made, and many advertisers do not want to be associated with the poor production quality.

The appeal among younger people may be fine if that's your target audience, but if you're seeking consumers who are older—and have more disposable income—you may not find these vehicles such a great match. Newsweeklies rely completely on the income they receive from advertising to cover production costs and salaries, so it's incumbent upon them to squeeze a many ads into as small a space as they can in order to reduce the overall cost of printing. This may not be beneficial to you as an advertiser.

The cost of ads in alternative newsweeklies varies, but usually they are one-eighth to one-fourth the cost of newspaper ads.

Place-Based/Point-of-Purchase

Place-based or point-of-purchase marketing goes back to the 1800s, according to Hampton Roads, when the legendary Smith Brothers first advertised their cough drops (and their portraits) on the counter of a general store. Today P-O-P marketing is everywhere. In grocery stores, you can find any number of useful, small items, plus a host of magazines, on your way through the checkout counter. Department and convenience stores offer the same types of items that appeal to the customer who will buy on impulse, on end caps in stores, shopping bags, items placed *outside* the store like seasonal plants at a grocery store, etc. Placement is limited only by the creativity of the marketing manager.

According to industry data, place-based advertising only reaches a small group of consumers, and apparently is best aimed at younger, less affluent shoppers.

Whole Health Expos and Other Trade Shows

I'm sure you are familiar with the whole health expos that have spread across the country. Expos are a wonderful way of meeting potential clients and networking with other therapists and members of the holistic community. In most cases, you rent an exhibit space, usually in a hotel or convention center, for a certain price. The size of the space varies and you can pay anywhere from $400 to $2,000 per booth, for a weekend. Some shows are two-day events, others just one day.

You or your partner, spouse, or friend, are expected to be available at your booth throughout the show, demonstrating your skills, providing information, and handing out your brochures and business cards. You can even charge a nominal fee for a 10-minute massage, Rolfing session, or whatever it is that you do. In addition, there may be an opportunity for you to speak at the expo in a one or two-hour session. These "platforms" give you a chance to talk about who can benefit from your practice or what particular ailments are especially improved by your skills.

Check the list of holistic health expos throughout the country and try to attend the nearest one to you before you sign on. Be sure to ask how many people are expected to walk through the door. What is the history of the event? What will be expected of you? Can you bring in family members for free? Try to anticipate the additional costs of rooms to stay in, food and drink throughout the weekend, etc.

Expos provide an excellent way to meet a crowd of people already open to your holistic craft, and to network with other bodyworkers from your region. You can learn a great deal about what's going on in your area by sharing information on rates, office rents, availability of conference halls for workshops, new techniques, etc. Expos also allow you to reach an audience you might not otherwise have access to, such as a visiting mother-in-law who is just there because her daughter brought her, but who ends up being fascinated by your healing magnets and buys a few.

The cost of participating in an expo can be high in some areas, and they can be physically draining. If you decide to participate, it would behoove you to arrange time to give a free lecture at the show and to advertise in the program guide for the event. Make sure you know exactly what to expect when you get there so you are not disappointed with the arrangements. If you are bringing something to heat your stones with, check with the producer of the show to make sure they have the electrical power to support your heater.

Summary

So what does all this mean for you? My recommendation for a practitioner just starting out would be to invest in newspaper and local magazine ads. In addition, take full advantage of free advertising like posting your business cards wherever they are welcome, and thumb tacking flyers with your name and phone number onto bulletin boards. As business grows, many practitioners find a radio ad very effective, and certainly a sandwich sign on the sidewalk outside your office would be great.

No doubt your first consideration will be your budget and how much you can afford at the start. Remember that the place you advertise (the local coffee shop bulletin board), or the vehicle in which you advertise (the local newspaper or magazine) is a reflection on you. Make certain that you want to be seen in these places, and that they will act to support your practice, not detract from it.

In addition to paid advertising, there are other things you can do to draw clients in that will not cost you anything. We'll take a look at those in the next chapter.

CHAPTER TEN

Catch 'Em
and Keep 'Em

Attracting and Retaining Clients

Once you've decided how you're going to advertise your business, consulted with a graphic artist, and secured a pricing quote from a printing company for business cards, brochures, and flyers, it's time to strategize for bringing in the clients. As I've stated before, you'll first want to pepper your community with business cards. I know someone who threw 50 cards out a third floor window, and watched as people on the busy street below picked them up. Most of them pocketed the card for future reference. The sky is the limit with creative ideas for distributing your printed wares.

Generally speaking, you want to look for places that have a high amount of foot traffic such as doctors' offices, hospital waiting rooms, libraries, coffee shops, restaurants, copying shops, community centers—even the corner drug store. Place your cards and flyers wherever community bulletin boards exist such as the YMCA, a recreational center, athletic facilities, gymnasiums, etc.

When you start out it can be scary to think of your competition out there on the streets and in the stores doing exactly what you're doing. Before you can grow your business, you must understand *and believe* that there really is enough business out there for everyone. Economists may say that's nonsense—that the concept of scarcity is a fact, and that there are only so many pieces of the market pie to go around. If you don't grab yours up, someone else will.

Whether this concept has validity or not, if you allow it to dominate your thoughts, you will never move forward. In the holistic community, we prefer to focus on the notion that there is enough for everyone—that abundance is possible for *all* practitioners. Why? Because each practice brings to it a unique individual with unique skills, training, and techniques; therefore each practitioner has a chance to carve out his or her own share of the market. With hard work and vigilance, you will be able to experience steady growth. I am not naïve enough to think that all of us are destined to be rich and successful. I have, however, experienced firsthand the power of positive affirmations with regard to business, and I've watched many other people succeed by believing in themselves, and "showing up" to make sure that the important aspects of their businesses have been properly addressed. When you do this, good things happen.

EXERCISE

This exercise has always worked for me. When I was approaching a deadline, I would sit quietly in a chair, close my eyes, and try to reach a state of total relaxation. Then I would envision a giant mushroom cloud of light that would shoot way up into the air above my city, and spread out all over my state. I pictured it gradually starting to fall around a wider circumference that included all of New England. The cloud would quietly land on people I wanted to round up for advertising in my magazine.

I did this several times during the course of the deadline period and I can honestly say I was never disappointed. I made sure, of course, that I had made all my phone calls, and sent out all my reminders, but those few times that I failed to do my mental visualizations, I did notice my advertising revenues dropping off. I don't know exactly why it works—I just know that it does.

If the mushroom cloud idea doesn't work for you, make up your own visualization. When you are working alone, it can be frightening at first to wait for your business to pick up. If you already have overdue bills, you can actually become somewhat panic-stricken if you let it get to you. This is where a focus on professional practices, coupled with reassuring visualizations, can bring you back to center and a sense of peace.

Again, another positive approach is to act "as if" you are already there—as if you already have a thriving practice with just the type of clients you've always wanted to attract. When Olympic hopefuls enter the final race, they have already seen themselves winning. They don't have any trouble imagining or believing that they will win. If they doubted themselves, they wouldn't be there in the first place.

"As if" can be a tough concept to grasp at first, but practice it every day as often as you can, and it will become easier. Gradually you'll watch it become reality. Because you are working alone, it's important to be able to steer your mind onto the right track all by yourself if it starts to wander off into the "What if?" zone, as in "What if I can't pay my bills?" Just don't go there. All that will do is increase your anxiety. Instead, ask yourself if you have covered all of your daily business tasks. Repeat a few positive affirmations, and create a new visualization to help you relax.

Developing and Tracking Leads

Distributing business cards and brochures is one way to develop leads. Another is to develop your own direct mailing list. You can do this by going through the Yellow Pages and recording the names, addresses, and phone numbers of people in your community with similar interests. In other words, if you are a massage therapist, you might want to note the names of the acupuncturists in your town. As people who already appreciate the benefits of holistic health practices, they very well might be up for a massage after work. Think about what audiences would benefit from *your* services. When you do a direct mailing that offers your special of the month, you can include them, thus introducing yourself and reinforcing your place in the local market. I often find brochures for massage in my chiropractor's office, and I've seen business cards for acupressure in a psychotherapist's office.

Another useful activity along these lines is driving around with a tape recorder. Anytime you're running errands around town, carry a mini recorder with you and have a blank tape ready. When you see a sign for a practice that might be of interest, dictate the name, phone (if it's on their sign), and address, and add that practice to your mailing list when you get back to the office. I found lots of new clients this way.

For the most part, people are surprised and happy to find themselves on your mailing list, even if they are competitors. Your inclusion of them reflects your honorable intentions of sharing the market wealth, and becoming an ally in good business practices.

Network Like a Fisherman

Networking with other practitioners can be extremely helpful. Often you'll find practitioners who want to share information about their client base, their rates, etc. You may also find someone who wants to share office space to cut down on costs. Another reason for networking with other practitioners is that they may start to refer clients to you. If, for example, you are a massage therapist who prefers to work on smaller people, you can refer the very large man on the other end of the phone to one of your colleagues who would be much more comfortable treating such a client. If soothing a shoulder with bursitis isn't your area of expertise as a massage therapist, perhaps you would send someone with this condition to a feldenkrais practitioner.

As I mentioned earlier, it's always a good idea to join your local, state, and or national association and remain in good standing by keeping your dues up to date. Through these organizations, you can find out about other people in your area and start to participate in organizational activities. Your local Chamber of Commerce is also a tremendous place to network. Many chambers offer a monthly after-work-hours social gathering where business cards are freely exchanged and information about the local business community is readily shared. It's a great way to meet people if you are new to your area.

Places to network are unlimited. You can chat it up at art exhibitions, concerts, church dinners, PTA meetings, open houses, conventions, opera intermissions—virtually anywhere people are gathered, and where the setting allows for casual conversation between strangers.

A Return Visit Guaranteed

Let's assume you've culled lots of names from all the places we've mentioned, you've sent out your flyer to your whole mailing list, and you're starting to get some calls. What can you do to cultivate your first-time clients and assure yourself of a return visit from them?

The first thing to do is to make your clients feel welcome. Treat them as you would a guest in your home. Always use your client's name when you greet him or her, and at some point during the course of a session. Even if your kids were late getting to school, and you had a flat tire on the way in to work, your job is to forget all that and put on a smile. It may seem hypocritical, but it will actually make you feel better anyway. Remember that one of the hallmarks of a holistic practice is attention to the overall needs of the individual. Focus on the person in front of you. There will be time later to cope with problems outside of work.

Having completed a session, go straight to your computer and make notes about the client who just left. First make a note about how they found you—the Yellow Pages, a newspaper ad, word-of-mouth, etc. Knowing the source helps you figure out what's working for you. Log the results into your database management software and tabulate it periodically. Have a reward system in place for clients who bring in other clients. Offer a free session for every three new clients one of your regular clients brings in.

Next, note the client's physical problems, important issues, and concerns. Don't wait until the end of the day to make your notes; it's too easy to forget little details when you're tired and ready to go home. No one wants to have to retell their whole story each time they come to see you. There truly is nothing worse than going back to see a practitioner for the second or third time, and having to remind them of your physical complaints, and what was done about them the last time. The perception in the client's mind at that point is that you, the practitioner, are not professional. You have not taken the time, or shown the interest required, either because you are lazy, disorganized or just plain incompetent. Even though your clientele may be a fairly relaxed and casual crowd in general, never assume it's okay to say something like, "It's been such a busy week. Remind me what we did last time?" In some states, it may even be illegal not to have written records of treatments.

Most people don't stop to think about how difficult it would be for you to remember each little detail of their last session, and they can become irritated with you for not remembering. We all want to feel special, particularly in this intimate setting. Be sure to check each client's file before he or she arrives for the next appointment, and scan it carefully for details. Remembering the least little thing can sometimes save you in the mind of the client. Again, attention to this kind of detail will build your practice.

Another thing you can do, as a favor to yourself *and* your clients, is call or email your clients with a reminder one or two days ahead of their appointment. This is very important if you want to cut down on missed appointments. People seem extraordinarily busy these days, and appointments can easily be forgotten. A phone call or an email along these lines also supports your position if the appointment does get missed anyway—at least you tried to remind them, and by calling before your own 24-hour cancellation timeframe, there can be no question about their obligation to pay.

Keep in mind that the success of your business depends on those people who come back to you again and again. Even if they come to you for a period of two years, and disappear for two more, they may very well come back after that when they require your services again. You never know, but return clients are worth cultivating in every possible way. Think about what one steady client can mean financially to your business. If you charge $70 an hour and see a client for massage once every three weeks (about 17 times a year), that amounts to $1,190 annually. If that client continues for two years, that would be $2,380, but the multiplicity that results from happy clients goes well beyond these numbers because of the referrals they make to their friends. Inevitably, your repeat clients will bring you, on average, another two or three new clients. Your original client may take advantage of your special promotions, buy gift certificates, and purchase some of your products, which further increases the amount of money they contribute to your practice. Assuming the new clients brought in by the original client do the same thing, it's not hard to understand why return business is so important.

Making Special Deals

I used to talk to literally hundreds of people in the course of one of my deadlines. I couldn't possibly remember everything I discussed with my clients, but if I made a special deal with someone I wrote it down in their invoice file so that I could say, "Oh yes, I did agree to that," or "I *do* remember that you wanted to get into the fall issue." As a business owner you have the prerogative to make special arrangements with your clients. If someone is experiencing hardship, you have the absolute right to give him or her a financial break, but if you do, remember to *write it down*. Forgetting a special deal, and possibly even questioning your client's credibility later on, is as negligent as forgetting their physical concerns.

Boosting Business in a Slump

If the business starts to fall off somewhat, what can you do to boost it back up? This is where your computer filing system can be invaluable. Let's say the winter dragged business-wise, and you need to jump start it. You can look up all the people who came in for a massage last spring. You are able to track them by date because that's the way you have set up your files. Send them a direct mailing about your spring special offerings, or call them up for a personal chat. Simply begin by saying, "It's been a while since I've seen you. How is your shoulder doing?" Let the client respond, then explain that you're calling to let them know about a special you're offering, or if you've been taking classes, a special technique you've just learned that would be very helpful for their condition.

Most people will welcome your call. The worst that can happen is they will say "no thank you," but frequently they will accept your offer and make an appointment. The client may even have been thinking of coming in to see you, but just never got around to it. I've heard this about a million times. Find a way to stay in touch with your clients.

Create a customer service survey, and ask your clients to take it home to fill it out. It isn't necessary for them to include their names if they don't wish to. All you're after is the feedback, and you might not get truthful answers if you require names.

Ask your colleagues and practitioners in other disciplines to observe your work. Listen to their comments and decide for yourself what is most useful. I know some acupuncturists who trade for services. One of them told me that when she went to her friend for acupuncture, she always requested the biggest, sharpest needles for treatment for what she perceived to be the biggest benefit. But when it was her friend's turn to experience acupuncture, she requested the smallest possible needles and said, "Can you believe we do this to people all day?" It's important to know that your clients sensitivities can vary, and maybe a colleague can point this out better than anyone.

Freebies: Demo's, Public Speaking, and Volunteering

There are other things you can do to draw clients in that can be very effective. They will cost you time and energy, but usually nothing more. Free demonstrations at shopping malls, recreation centers, gymnasiums, and outdoor events, are a wonderful way to introduce your community to your work. You can also volunteer for charitable organizations that offer support to the friends and family members of seriously ill patients. One such organization where I live is called Cancer Connection, which offers a network of support for people who have just been diagnosed with cancer. It provides information, free classes on everything from quilting to rowing, and offers free holistic treatments like Reiki. Organizations like this also provide the perfect opportunity for you as a practitioner to demonstrate your expertise, and to perform useful services free-of-charge. Your unselfish contributions to these organizations and associations do not go unnoticed—by the community or the universe—so don't hesitate to schedule some time with them. Word of your expertise will get out.

Another way to promote your work is to do some public speaking. Contact your Chamber of Commerce for ideas about groups and organizations who might be interested in hearing about your occupation. Rotary clubs, and charitable organizations like the Elks, the BPOE, and the Knights of Columbus are frequently looking for speakers for their monthly luncheons. Tie your practice into the business community by talking about the business aspects of your field. After explaining what cranial manipulation is, explain how your practice contributes to the local economy. Hospitals, nursing homes, and high school sports teams might appreciate learning more about your massage techniques, and local elementary school teachers might benefit from knowing how your sand play therapy works. You never know when someone may be looking for a service just like yours, either for themselves or for someone they know. You can design your talk to fits the needs of the organization while using it as a launching pad for your practice.

Many of the same organizations mentioned above are looking for attractions for their fund-raising events. Volunteer to help promote a cause by contributing your services. Offer free massages for increments of 15-minutes throughout the event. It will be a tough day, but think how many people you will have introduced to your skills.

You can also make some extra money by holding seminars. Let's say you've been in business for a couple years, and you'd like to do some more networking, and spread some of your own knowledge through the community. You could rent a space in a conference center, hotel, or college classroom (sometimes these are free), and hold a seminar for a number of other people in your field who might be interested in what you've accomplished with your business. Everyone's looking for opportunities to connect, and to glean some helpful tips. If you charged $100 for an all-day seminar and gathered 25 people from around your city or state, you'd probably net upwards of $1,500. One way to attract people to a seminar is hire a well-known speaker in the field. This would cut down on your profit, but profit may not be your only goal. Becoming known in your field in your own community and/or state is no small accomplishment. Becoming known to your colleagues, as you would through an article you publish in a trade journal, is also something that can never hurt you, and will benefit your practice.

Press Releases

Another way to round up some new folks is to send a press release to the editor of the newspaper in your area. Newspapers can have several editors—the sports editor, the features editor, the city desk editor, and the calendar editor—so if you don't know which one to send it to, and don't know his or her name, call the paper to get it before sending in the release.

A press release is an announcement of a new product, service, event, or grand opening. Perhaps in your case, you would be announcing your arrival in town and the opening of your new office. Below is an example of a press release. Most press releases follow a particular format. You can certainly write the release yourself, but understand that they have certain components that you want to incorporate in order to adhere to a professional standard. The top right-hand corner will indicate your name and contact information. The first line contains the name of your business; the second line contains the street address of your business; the third line contains your city, state and zip code; the fourth contains the date; and the fifth contains your contact information. Be sure to print the word "CONTACT" in bold capitals followed by all the ways you can be reached—email, phone, website, fax, telescope—whatever. Editors are very busy people, often inundated with reading material so you want to make it very easy for them to find what they need quickly.

The information above is followed on the far left-hand side of the page by the words: FOR IMMEDIATE RELEASE. This is code for "Please print this as soon as possible." The second line contains the name of the editor (usually a feature editor, but this can vary with different newspapers). The third line contains the name of the newspaper, the fourth line contains the street address of the newspaper, and the fifth contains the newspaper's city, state and zip code.

Now you've arrived at the most critical part: the headline. This will be the hook that either snags or gags the editor so it has a big job to do. Think about your angle. What is it about your work that would be of interest to your community? Do you do something really unusual? Are you introducing a new form of massage or psychotherapy to the area? Do you have the latest equipment or gadget in your field? Next translate whatever you come up with into a clever title.

Puns can be a great way to attract an editor's attention, but you need a good one, a clever one—not the kind of pun that makes people sigh and shake their heads—and don't use clichés. The headline shown in the sample is an example of a good pun. Get your friends and family involved. This headline could mean the difference between publication or the trash can, so put some time into it.

Once you've established a real eye-catcher of a headline, center it on the page following the newspaper information on the left-hand side. Now comes the story. The first line will begin with what's called a "dateline" (which is really a place line) as you can see from the upper and lower case words "Florence, MA."

When telling your story in a press release, you want to follow a particular order. The standard order of information for journalism is who, what, where, when, and how, but feature articles can bend the rules a little. Just highlight the main message in the first paragraph. When describing the action, the product, or the new workshop, get a quote from someone in a position to know something about your subject.

Figure out where you are most likely to get a positive quote. Let's say you've just had tremendous success with a client who had a foot problem. You know that this person was going to a podiatrist about the pain that would not go away. When the doctor sees that the pain has been greatly decreased due to your massage, the podiatrist might be inclined to say something like, "Yes, I was surprised by the results of Mr. Heel Pain's massage." When you get a quote from someone, ask the person if he or she would mind if you use the quote. Be sure to get the correct spelling of the name and identify the person accurately in the release. Editors like an authoritative quote because it gives weight to the story. Most people are willing to offer a short quote for the paper, but even if the person is a public figure, be sure to ask for permission to use the quote.

Figure 10-1.

Cancer Connection, Inc.
P. O. Box 60452
Florence, MA 01062
April 3, 2000
CONTACT: Deb Orgera
413/586-1642

FOR IMMEDIATE RELEASE
Ms. Get Name, Feature Editor
Daily Hampshire Gazette
115 Conz Street
Northampton, MA 01060

PULLING TOGETHER:
Beginning Rowers Sought for Cancer Connection Program

Florence, MA (April 3, 2000)—Everyone who has faced a diagnosis of any type of cancer can benefit from the support of others like them. Now a new initiative will enable some area residents with cancer to recognize that they are all in the same boat—quite literally.

The Cancer Connection Rowing Program will be launched this month at an orientation meeting on Tuesday, April 11. The aim of this non-competitive program is "to offer an opportunity for people living with or recovering from cancer to enjoy a physical activity and learn the sport of rowing, as well as to get to know each other, share experiences and simply have fun," says volunteer coach Betsy Powell.

"I expect about eight to 12 individuals—both men and women—to take part," explains Powell, whose credentials include crew-coaching posts at Smith College, Mount Holyoke College, and Tufts and Syracuse universities. "It's an introductory-level program," she stresses, "so no experience is necessary, although all rowers must be able to swim and get a doctor's okay to take part."

Some details about the new venture have not yet been finalized. It will run between four to eight weeks in June and July, says Powell, with sessions three times per week on the Connecticut River, based at the Smith College boat house in Hadley. The college is donating the use of its facility and equipment. Exact dates and times will depend on participants' schedules, notes Powell, "but I promise there will be no early mornings, unless, of course, the rowers want them!"

The April 11 gathering will be held at 5 p.m. at the Silk Mill, 269 Locust Street, Florence. Prospective participants can meet Powell and each other, discuss program specifics, and hear about "pre-season training" activities.

Cancer Connection, Inc. is a new local resource center for people diagnosed with cancer and their families. According to co-founders Deb Orgera and Jackie Walker, this rowing group will be unique to the region. It is loosely modeled on a similar program in western Canada that Orgera learned about at a recent conference. Cancer Connection has previously sponsored such courses and workshops as "Skills for Coping" and "Painting for Joy," with additional offerings now being planned. For more information, contact Cancer Connection at 413-586-1642.

-30-

Press releases should not go over a single page in length unless there is a very compelling reason. All press releases end with the number 30, preceded and followed by a dash. If for any reason you must use two pages, the end of the first page should have the word "more" centered at the bottom of the page, preceded and followed by a dash.

Send the letter to the appropriate editor or deliver it in person. If you decide to deliver it in person, be very brief in describing your release. If you haven't heard anything from the editor in a week, call or email the person, and politely ask if you can answer any questions. Try to figure out if there is any interest in your story. Press releases are an absolutely fabulous way to "advertise" because they cost nothing, but are read by thousands of people. It's worth one more call to check with an editor, but don't go beyond that, or you might ruin your chances with that editor for a future release. If during your first phone call, the editor explains that he or she just hasn't had time to get to it, wait another week and call again. If the editor waffles and says something like, "I'm just not sure this is for us," don't push it. Leave the door open by indicating you'd be happy to contribute something more to their liking in the future. Thank them for their time and let them go. You've left a positive impression by not pushing or wasting their time with a sales pitch. In the interim, read the releases that come out in the paper and try to get a better feel for what might fly the next time around.

See Figure 10-1 sample press release.

Query Letters

Another wonderful freebie is an article written by you placed in the feature section of your local newspaper, in a magazine, or in a trade journal. In this case you will want to send what's called a query letter to the feature editor. A query letter is an enticement from you to the editor and should be *no longer than one page*. If the editor is interested, they will contact you and ask for the whole article. Again, call to get his or her name. Never send the article with the query letter unless expressly asked to do so.

There is a very particular format for query letters that differs from press releases. And, there is a different type of query letter for articles than for books, or soliciting agents. The address on the top right is yours, and the one on the left is theirs just as in a standard business letter.

The first paragraph should be a very catchy way of telling the editor what brought your attention to their paper and should explain the premise of the article. This paragraph should be followed by one (or possibly two) paragraph(s) of the *actual article* to demonstrate your writing skill.

The next paragraph (paragraph 3) should explain what you can provide in this article, for example:

I can provide a 2,000-5,000-word article on infant massage that will include:

- The enormous benefits of massage therapy to infants
- Steps to ensure that you've chosen the right massage therapist
- How infant massage shortens time of illness
- Teaching mothers how to perform infant massage at home and so on.

The paragraph that follows (paragraph 4) should tell what qualifies you to write the article—what your background is, where you've trained, what degrees and certifications you hold, and how long you've been doing this work. Finally, in the last paragraph you will provide contact information.

Query letters can be a real challenge to write. As you can see, you have to fit a lot of information into a very small space. It needs to be very concise. Think of a query letter in the same way you would running out of the house if it was in flames—you'd grab only the most essential items on your way out—kids, spouse, the dog, photographs, and you're out of there. Any extraneous material is unwelcome by an editor because it just takes up their time. In this way, a query letter is very similar to selling a screenplay. You have only ten minutes to pitch the film, and the script can only be 120 pages long. Anything longer or shorter can get canned automatically. It's a way the industry weeds out the professionals from the amateurs.

Though tricky to write, query letters can pay off big time if your article gets published. Any efforts on your part to contribute further information to the public, underscores your level of professionalism and is a great way to advertise for free.

Summary

Use your creativity to develop visualizations for attracting new clients and use them frequently. Network like crazy in every possible setting. Make notes about any special deals you make with your clients so that you'll have a reference to check. Take advantage of the many free ways to advertise your business such as demonstrations, volunteer activities, public speaking, press releases and query letters.

CHAPTER ELEVEN

The Common Woes of
Sole Proprietors

We've covered virtually all the components of your practice except one: *you*. Here you are—directing your own life by working independently of a company, an institution or a boss. Congratulations! The increased independence of your sole proprietorship can give you an enormous sense of self-determination and control over how you spend your time—when you work, how many days you take off, when you go on vacation and so on. Perhaps you chose your current work as a result of downsizing or not wanting to relocate, or you may simply have decided you could no longer work for someone else. In any case, you are now relying on your own mental, physical and financial resources to provide for yourself and your family. This can be very liberating, but it can also be lonely and even exhausting when you are the only person responsible for making your business work—and you *are* a business.

Without the support of a business partner or an incorporated group, which we will discuss later in this chapter, you alone are shouldering the burden of acquiring clients, doing the bookkeeping, cleaning your office, updating your records, and a million other essential tasks, in addition to practicing your profession. It can be a lot to handle. Unfortunately, it's often the case that the people who give the most to others through physical or mental care, are the last to take care of themselves.

If you want to be successful at maintaining your business equanimity, which includes your mental and spiritual health, you must apply practical means for coping with the steady buildup of day-to-day stress. Because you never know exactly what any given day will bring, it's important to find ways of developing resilience and flexibility. It's hard, for example, to keep up your end of a conversation with a client when you have a sick child at home if you have not established for yourself a regular means of de-stressing. Remember the tortoise and the hare? Slow, steady and *centered* will win this race. If practiced on a regular basis, the following simple little techniques can extend your energy and allow you to approach your career with enthusiasm most, if not all, of the time.

Keep in mind that the methods you choose to take care of your own well-being are not as important as just making sure you are doing so holistically—caring for your own body, mind and spirit—in ways that are in sync with your own practices and beliefs. Healing should begin with a healer who is well.

Recognizing Burnout

First, in order to avoid burnout, you have to be able to recognize what it is and what it feels like before it begins to drag you down. If you find your energy level flagging, or find that you can't sleep at night, or that you're letting the paperwork side of the business slide—STOP. Sit down and ask yourself if you have taken on too much. Are you seeing too many clients in too short a period of time just to keep your cash flow moving? If you are a massage therapist, have you been working on people who are really too large for you to handle on a regular basis? If you are a physical therapist, are all your rotator cuff patients starting to seem alike? Ask yourself this question: "Am I giving my best effort to every client I have?"

If the answer is no, then you need to look at the ways you can cut back and regroup. One way to do this is to build into each day a time at the beginning and at the end for meditation. This could take as little as ten minutes just to relax and embrace the day at the beginning of work, and ten more to release the stress at the end of it. You don't need to do anything other than just sit quietly in a chair with your eyes closed, breath deeply, and practice letting go of whatever it is that is causing you to feel dragged under. Clear out the mental cobwebs and refresh your perspective.

Depending on what kind of a week you're having, twice a day may not be enough. Many massage therapists, who need to give their hands and arms a rest, and many psychotherapists, who need to give their heads a rest, factor in a brief time between clients to meditate and de-stress. Only you can be the judge of whether or not this would be helpful to you, but if you have any doubts, remember to ask yourself if you are giving your best effort to every client you have. Meditation should leave you feeling revived and ready. If you are too rushed or too overwhelmed with your workload, you will not experience these feelings.

Meditation Exercise

Sit in a comfortable chair and rest your feet flat on the floor. Close your eyes and take a deep breath. Continue to breath deeply and focus on each intake and exhalation. Start at the top of your head and imagine light, white energy beginning to flow down through your body. The energy spreads very slowly through your forehead and down through your neck. Let it continue to flow down through your shoulders and imagine that each muscle in your shoulders is gradually letting go of its tension. Keep your limbs loose and follow the path of the energizing light as it finally reaches your toes. Slowly come back into the world and remember what relaxation feels like.

I can't say often enough, or strongly enough, how important I find this exercise. It took me a long time before I would give it the validation it deserves, but I used it regularly at times of extreme stress and I think it saved me from developing major problems. Sometimes, however, even taking a breather doesn't do the job completely. If this is the case for you, and one day you find yourself feeling extremely frustrated or beleaguered, especially if one or more of your clients are driving you nuts, get in your car and go to the carwash for a visual meditation. This is actually a lot of fun.

The Carwash

You want the kind of carwash you drive through without having to do a thing. As the car progresses along the track, think about how safe and dry you are as the soap and water assault the windows. Watch how the cloths designed to clean the sides flap back and forth furiously as you sit there completely untouched by them. Pay attention to how you feel as the car starts to pull back out into the sunlight. You want to retain for your visceral memory the feeling you experienced as you went through this process. The world can throw whatever it will at you, but you need to remain unfazed by it. That is not to say that you won't have reactions to the things that happen in your life. It is to say that you don't want to lose your center in the process. Remain calm knowing that you can handle whatever, or whoever, it is and will do so in your own time and in your own way.

The Washer/Dryer Exercise

In any business, managing people in general, and dealing with some clients in particular, can prove to be a challenge. Office politics, gossip, and maneuvering for position are often the source of stress and strain. An exercise for dealing with specific clients can be played out mentally by focusing on your washer and dryer. Let's say you have a very fussy client who nonetheless comes back on a regular basis and contributes to the financial security of your operation. You don't want to eliminate this person from your practice, but you have to find a way to cope with her constant demands and apparent insensitivity to your needs. What do you do?

Stuff her in the washer! Not literally, of course, but mentally visualize popping Mrs. R. U. Whining into the washer for a good soak. Imagine her reaction as you squelch her squalking and force her to sit there in the lukewarm water and think about her bad behavior. Is she apologetic? Does she get it yet? You may find at this point you actually have some empathy for her. Maybe she's not so bad after all. In this case, you can let her out. It's a good sign that you will remember this feeling of empathy the next time she comes into your office. As she begins to do her number, you can just think of how it felt to see her dripping wet.

If she's still fuming and you don't have any empathy yet, then it's time to get her full attention with the aggressive agitation of the wash cycle. Add soap to wash out all her poisonous words and actions. Ask the universe to show her the ways of kindness as you watch her flatten out around the edges during the spin cycle, rendering her quite helpless and pitiful. Pop her in the dryer and set it on Permanent Pest! Imagine that this particular setting extracts any vestige of hostility from your currently whirling client. Bless her as she emerges from the dryer all nice and clean and fluffy. Wish her well, she's had a tough time. As many of us know, difficult people become difficult as a result of a lack of love or attention, or both, somewhere along the way. Let the washer/dryer exercise remind you that we all have our shortcomings and can use a good "cleaning" once in awhile.

I performed this mental exercise with a client who was really exasperating. The next time I talked to her on the phone, I burst out laughing. I kept picturing her in the spin cycle and I'd just crack up. I couldn't tell her why I was laughing, but she started laughing too. I managed to get my composure back and we had a very nice conversation. After that I honestly never encountered the same feeling of frustration in dealing with her. My attitude toward her had changed and the incident left a deep impression on me.

Exercise Can Make A Difference

Meditation and the exercises above will address your mental health, but you should not discount the need for physical relief as well. Even massage therapists who are physically active all day can benefit from some form of exercise, like walking, to reduce the amount of stress that can build up in a day's time. Here, the choices are endless. Yoga is an all-time favorite because of its renown de-stressing effects and it's muscle strenghtening capability. But what if you are a yoga teacher and have been practicing it all day? Perhaps for you something aerobic is the trick. It's amazing how aerobic exercise can take you to a different place in very short order. As much as you may not feel like doing any exercise after work, it's highly likely you will feel better after having taken even a short walk.

Massage, as you know, is also an essential tool for releasing stress and tension in the muscles. If you can't afford to schedule a regular massage right now, find another therapist you can trade with. Having buddies in the business is a huge advantage here. You might also consider a support group including other people in your profession who get together on a regular basis to talk shop. Doing so will increase your knowledge of your craft while fulfiling some of your socializing needs at the same time.

Acupressure and Rolfing are also wonderful stress relievers. Learn some acupressure points for those times when you can feel tension building in particular parts of your body. If you start to get a headache, for example, use the thumb and forefinger of your left hand to squeeze the skin at the base of your right thumb just where it meets your right index finger.

Chiropractic adjustments are my medicine of choice for those times when I'm aware of having held my body in a particular position for a long time. I spend a lot of time at my computer. I often find at the end of a day that I've been leaning forward with my neck extended, leaving a knot in my upper back. Massage therapists who are reaching over a bodywork table all day would no doubt benefit from a few spinal tweaks at some point.

In addition to the few modalities I've mentioned here, there are many others that would be of help, and many other ways of pairing and sharing services with other practitioners (see the list of holistic practices in Chapter 1). A day at a spa, a week at a retreat, and just plain rest away from work can also be invigorating. Sometimes all it takes to get your energy back is a quick trip out of town or a weekend away somewhere. Make sure you don't answer your phone. Give yourself the time to leave the work behind and recuperate.

Another excellent method of destressing is biofeedback. With the use of a mechanical instrument and electrodes attached to you, you can learn to sense when your muscles are tensing, and even when your blood pressure is rising. With this knowledge, you can stop stress in its tracks by first recognizing when its affecting you physically, and then by practicing deep breathing exercises, meditation, guided imagery, and other techniques aimed at calming the body and mind.

Another way to accomplish a quick "calm down" is to employ a deep yoga breath. This involves all the deep muscles of the diaphram, belly, and lungs. First inhale as slowly as possible, through your stomach by allowing it to extend outward, then by your lungs allowing them to fill to their fullest extent. Then exhale in the same slow way. At first you may find it difficult to breathe in to a slow count of 12, and exhale to the same count. but keep at it. Even trying to get to that number will be useful in terms of stress leaving your body, and bringing oxygen to your brain and nervous system.

In addition to caring for your body and mind, it's important to make sure you are seeing friends and family members on a regular basis for your own social well-being. As a sole proprietor you may not experience the same camaraderie that office workers often do since you are by yourself all day. For you, coffee breaks, or moments with a cup of chai, don't usually involve chatting around the water cooler with your co-workers. You may need to initiate contact with your friends in order to see them on a regular basis. Make a list of friends you can invite to lunch or meet for after-work drinks. I keep my list visible on my computer and make sure that I either call or make a date with one of them at least once a week. When I've worked my way down the list, I start over. This process helps me keep track of the people who are important to me. I never want to let too much time or distance come between us because I derive an enormous amount of spiritual sustenance from my friends.

If you are new in town and do not have a lot of contacts to start with, join a spiritual support group to meet other people with whom you have something in common. Sometimes just joining a group such as a writing workshop or an art class can give you the sense that you are participating in the world outside of your job.

What If It's All Just Too Much?

If you've attempted to relieve the stress you're encountering with meditation and exercise, and still find yourself struggling to keep your chin up, you can begin to explore other possibilities. You might, for example, decide to hire someone to help you out. This person could be a part-time employee who does a minimal amount of work for you amounting to only a couple hours a week, or someone you employ full-time to take on all the things you really don't want to have to deal with.

Your first consideration will be whether or not you can afford to pay someone else. If you can, and you decide to do so, you must know the laws regarding employees. You cannot just ask your Aunt Alice to help out and pay her in cash under the table. If you employ someone else even part-time, there are very specific guidelines you must follow with regard to taxes and the law. Never agree to pay an employee in cash and remember, it is a federal offense to hide any income. If you pay someone in cash and they fail to report it, you may think that is just their problem, but it doesn't stop there. If it is ever discovered that you participated in making cash payments on a regular basis, you yourself could be liable. Also, you are doing the person no favor by paying them in cash since they can be in serious trouble if they get caught. You also lose out on legitimate business write-offs because there is no "paper trail" in the form of cancelled checks or bank transactions verifying your payments.

It can be tempting when you're up against a financial wall to cut corners in this way, but my advice is don't do it. Number one, it's wrong. Number two, it's still wrong, so just don't attach yourself to bad practices from the beginning.

Hiring Help

If you decide to hire someone, that person will either be considered an employee or an independent contractor, each of which has tax implications. It is not necessary, for example to provide independent contractors with benefits, or to pay taxes for them; whereas in the case of an employee, you are required to pay social security tax (FICA), and worker's compensation.

The IRS has a very strict interpretation of what constitutes an employee and what does not. If you fail to report the correct status, you will be liable for fines and may have to pay back taxes. The basic categories are part-time employees, full-time employees, hourly employees, salaried employees, and independent contractors. If you are thinking about hiring an employee, it's best to consult a professional to make sure you are complying with the law and have the correct forms to fill out regarding compensation for that employee. Ask for a definition of your employee's status in writing from the professional you consult.

If you hire someone to assist you, and pay them more than $600 per year, you must report that fact to the IRS and provide the person you employ with a Form 1099 indicating the amount you've paid through the year. Talk to your accountant about your decision to hire, and ask for his or her advice on dealing with the attendant paperwork.

Partnerships and Corporations

Other business arrangements beside that of sole proprietor are partnerships and corporations. These are legal terms that describe how monies that come in will be divvied, up and have implications for liability as well. Sole proprietors are completely liable for any business-related problems, however, their tax rate is lower than that of partnerships and corporations, and the paperwork is much less extensive. Therefore, many if not most, holistic practitioners start out as sole proprietors, and hope that the insurances they have taken out will cover any costs that arise from negligence or malpractice.

A partnership involves two people who split the income, expenses, and liabilities of a company. Partnerships often turn out to be the bad boys of business relationships. Friends and relatives can start out in business and do just fine with each other until it's time to allocate funds. Another common problem is that one person has more energy, or is willing to do more work, than the other. Accusations and resentment along these lines can fester and may ultimately lead to the dissolution of the business.

On the other hand, a partnership for a massage therapy practice might work wonderfully for mothers who want to spend some time at home, yet don't want to be solely responsible for the practice. There are many advantages to this kind of arrangement because it can accommodate two lives with a single practice. The thing to know before you jump in is that it's important to make sure your lawyer has drawn up a very good and fair agreement between you and your partner so that if one of you opts out at some point, your half of the operation will not be totally lost.

What to Do if You're Sick

Even practicing all the healthy habits you can—exercising and eating properly—you may not be able to escape things like the flu or a bad cold. If you should get sick, you'll need to have a plan in place for coping with an absence from your office. One way to handle this situation is to ask colleagues in your field to accept your patients temporarily while you are ill, in return for accepting theirs if they should become sick. You may want to create a circle of people with whom you could make such a trade. Whatever you do, don't wait until you get sick, or need to have surgery, to do this.

If yours is not a practice in which you can easily pass your clients over to someone else, you'll need to contact your clients, explain the situation, and refer them to emergency services if their needs are urgent. Give them a realistic idea of when you expect to return to work, and when you might be able to schedule another appointment with them.

Naturally time off from your job will mean a loss of income, even if only temporarily. This is when business and/or disability insurance can prove to be such essential components of your business.

A Typical Day: All's Well that Starts Well

Let's walk through a typical day in your practice. Assuming you get to the office at 8:00 a.m. on Monday morning and your first client arrives at 9:00 a.m., you have an hour to get something else done. My recommendation is that you spend that time listening to messages from your phone answering service, pay any outstanding bills, catch up on other paperwork, make computer entries to your bookkeeping program or client files, and back up your computer information. Return any urgent calls and save the rest for the lunch hour. Now is also a good time to check your advertising calendar for approaching deadlines, and your tickler file for anything you might need to do that day. Does your office need cleaning? Figure out what day this week you're going to clean it. All this should take about half an hour. If you do these things on a regular daily basis, you won't have to worry about facing a huge pile of work later on in the week, or month.

Once you've finished, take ten minutes to check your notes on your first client. Put the information away, sit back in a comfortable chair and take a deep breath. Allow yourself to relax and contemplate your plans for that client. Ten to twenty minutes of meditation at the beginning of the day helps you switch gears from doing busy paper work (left brain activity) to focusing on the slower, more creative application of your craft (right brain activity). This exercise in relaxation also enables you to appear relaxed, confident, and ready when your client arrives.

If you charge for your services by the hour, schedule your time so that you can stop five or ten minutes before the hour ends to allow the client to get dressed or relax, while you pull up your next client's file. Give yourself enough time between clients so that you can review client files, refresh yourself, clean anything that needs to be cleaned from the last client, and spend a moment or two in meditation.

It will take a while before you can know exactly how many clients you are comfortable seeing in a day. At first it will be tempting to see as many as possible, but beware of over tiring yourself. If you are a massage therapist seeing more clients than your own physiology can comfortably handle, start scheduling more time in between for the muscles in your fingers and arms to recover. If you are a psychotherapist with an especially taxing load of clients with emotional traumas, schedule the greater number of clients in the morning, and allow yourself to unwind a little more in the afternoon. Recuperation of your physical, mental, and spiritual resources is essential if you are to continue to give care to your clients in the way that you want do.

Now let's assume you've seen three people this morning. Your first client came at 9:00 a.m. and your second client's appointment time was 10:15. You gave your first client five minutes at the end of the hour to regroup which left you with 15 minutes to read your next client files, clean up, and relax for a total of 20 minutes between clients. Following a similar schedule for your third client, you scheduled him for 11:30, finishing up at 12:30 (including the five minutes at the end of his session.)

Now you have an hour and a half for lunch from 12:30 p.m. to 2:00 p.m. This amount of time allows you to meet a friend for lunch, run a few quick errands, make some return phone calls, and review your 2:15 p.m. client's file. Working alone removes you from the every day hustle and bustle of the world, so it is important to maintain contact with your friends. Try to meet a friend for lunch at least once a week. If you do this, you won't mind the other days when you're in your office eating alone. In fact this time can be very valuable in terms of catching up on business details, and also for just having the time to yourself. If you have access to a shower, you might use this time to exercise three days a week.

For the afternoon, you've scheduled two clients—one at 2:15 p.m. and one at 3:30 p.m. The last client leaves your office shortly after 4:30 p.m. What do you do at this point? This part is really important because when you're tired at the end of the day, it can be so tempting to just hop in the car and go home. Before you do, you want to adopt the actions that will separate you from the people who fail at maintaining their sole proprietorship. Take an additional 15 minutes to look around the office and think about what needs to be done the next day. Are there phone calls you could be returning right now? Make a short list of the things you need to do in the morning. Then, once you're satisfied that you've covered your needs for the next day, sit down and meditate again for several minutes, allowing your body and mind to relax and relinquish the stress of the day. Use the exercise mentioned earlier that started your day, or develop another one for the end of the day. If you're feeling especially tense, put on some soothing music, and just listen quietly until you can feel the tension leave your muscles.

During this meditation, tell yourself that all pent-up stress and anxiety for that day is slowing draining away into the floor and out the door. You are finished with it and can start afresh tomorrow. When you're ready to get up, offer a prayer of gratitude for the wonderful day you've had. Incorporate as many nice things as you can think of that took place during the day, and genuinely thank the universe for your ability to participate in this life and contribute positively to the well-being of others. This daily practice will support your inner strength, reinforcing an unwavering conviction that carries you through your practice day after day.

What Else Can You Do?

Another way to foster the strength of your practice is to make a habit of reading up on the latest techniques in your field. Subscribe to several magazines and trade journals that feature articles about your specialty. Even if you don't actually learn these techniques immediately, you will at least have heard of them and have some knowledge of what they entail. At least once a year, try to schedule a time to take a class that teaches new techniques, or one that will enhance your other skills. The more knowledgeable you are, the more confidant you will be with your clients.

Avoid the Pitfalls

When you're just getting started in your practice, you have a ton of energy. It's very exciting to meet your clients, set up your office, and make all your arrangements. As time goes on, however, you may find your energy waning. You may discover, for example, you no longer feel like doing paperwork; or, you don't want to work on just anybody; or that you are certain you can cut costs by eliminating the professionals who are helping you with tax and legal issues. Here are some common mistakes that business owners make and what you can do to avoid them.

Don't Take on More Than You Can Handle

As a massage therapist, in the beginning you may decide to use your skills on anyone who walks in the door. Eventually you realize you are much more effective with women (or with men), or perhaps you are a small person yourself, and don't think you are providing adequately for the needs of your larger clients. If you are a psychotherapist, you may find yourself drawn to clients with a history of abuse; or you may decide you can't listen to one more adult and decide you're much more effective with children instead. In these cases, you may decide to specialize in order to sculpt a particular type of practice, filling it with the kind of people you really want to treat, and for whom your practice is most effective.

Pay Yourself First

This can be tough to do in the beginning because of course you need to pay your most urgent bills in order to stay afloat. After you've done so, even if its only five dollars, sock it away into a savings account. You never know when you'll need it, but more importantly, you want to establish this practice as a solid habit so that you will begin to build some capital. You'll want to pour money back into your practice for supplies, new equipment, and courses on new techniques, and if you continue to put away even a small amount of income for a "rainy day," you'll be pleasantly surprised to find how it grows.

Don't Let Your Paperwork Build Up
Don't Let Your Supplies Get Too Low

If you fail to address your paperwork, including insurance forms, tax forms, ledger entries, filing, correspondence—anything related to your business—you will regret it. It is much easier to address a stack of five papers versus a mountain of 500. If you don't, at tax time you might have to go through a whole year of information in order to provide your accountant with what is needed. Paperwork is invariably the part of business that everyone dislikes, so do as little as possible every day—but do it *every* day.

With regard to supplies, keep regular track of what's going where, and how many of each of your supplies are needed. Allow plenty of delivery time for essentials to arrive. Try to develop business accounts with your vendors so that you can be billed for supplies. If money is tight, you can make often arrangements for partial repayment until you receive the funds you need to cover them.

Stay on Top of Advertising and Marketing

Check your advertising information for any changes you might need to make. Also check your advertising calendar to make sure you're not missing deadlines. Even if you have several word-of-mouth regulars, you want to keep your name out there in case their numbers diminish—people move, they get fired and can't spend money on your services—anything can change your client picture sooner than you may wish.

Keep Your Professional Help

It can be very tempting to cut your lawyer, accountant, and computer technician out of your budget, but until you are absolutely certain you can manage their tasks by yourself, hang onto them.

Never Take Your Business for Granted

No matter how successful you become, your business will never be able to run by itself; it will always require your vigilance. At times, this can make you feel like a slave to the process of running it day in and day out, but there is no way around this simple fact. If you're exhausted by it, take a week off to rest and play. Try to focus on how happy you are to have a successful business, knowing that you could be working for a demanding boss in the traditional nine to five rat race.

Plan Your Schedule and Eliminate Time Wasters

Failing to plan results in having to scramble frantically to bring everything up to date later on. If you find yourself filling out nuisance questionnaires, or fiddling with a leaking toilet tank to no avail, stop! If a friend calls you at work and won't get off the phone, have your professional response ready: "I'm at work right now, and I have to get off the phone. I'd be happy to finish this conversation later." Don't waste your time on useless activities. If you need help fixing, moving, or doing something that seems to be taking way too long, call a friend, a plumber—whomever—and ask for help.

Learn from Your Mistakes
and Appreciate Your Accomplishments

You might like to think that once you've been in business for a few years, there are no more mistakes to make, but think again. The important thing to take away from whatever problem you created is the lesson it provides. Don't ruminate over it. Just acknowledge it, think about why it happened, how you can avoid such things in the future, and move on.

Try to place your emphasis on the things you've accomplished. For some people this is very hard since their mistakes seem to loom larger than their positive actions, even though their perception is probably distorted. Did you ever inadvertently insult someone, for example? I know a psychotherapist who was describing her work in a mental hospital at a party, saying, "I spend my whole day in a loony bin." The people to whom she was speaking had a son who had suffered a nervous breakdown. When she found this out, she was mortified. She apologized to the couple, but even though they were understanding and reassuring, she continued to feel terrible about the episode. Unfortunately, it may take mistakes like this before you develop some censorship on your own comments. Again, examine it, let it go, and try to focus on some of your business milestones.

Go Back to Your Original Goals

From time to time, go back to the original goals you set for yourself and your business. Do they still seem relevant? Are there new goals you might want to add? How close are you, or were you, to your one-year, three-year, and five-year projections? Reassess your goals even if business is sailing along. If things are going well, congratulate yourself and enjoy every bit of the credit you deserve. If not, maybe it's time to rethink your strategies. It's never too late to make changes; change is an integral part of keeping your business alive and vital.

Celebrate!

At least once a year, maybe on your birthday or your business anniversary, take some time to fully accept the incredible fact that you run your *own* business. This should be a somewhat different process than relishing your business accomplishments mentioned above. This is bigger. You had the dream, you did the work, you made it happen, and unlike many other people, you survived! A quirk of fate caused my business anniversary (the day I bought my business), to be April 1st—April Fool's Day. Every year on that day I would pinch myself and think, "This is no joke. It actually happened!"

Revel in your independence, knowing that you are contributing wonderful things to the world by helping other people, and increasing the well-being of humanity.

Summary

It's important to recognize and avoid burnout. Try to incorporate practices like meditation into your daily routine, and exercise into your weekly routine, to help relieve stress and eliminate the buildup of tension throughout your body. Take time to rest and relax between clients, find time to socialize with your friends and colleagues, and pay particular attention to your family's need for your presence. Check your original goals periodically to see how far you've come and where you might want to go in the future. Avoid the common mistakes of business owners by keeping a close eye on your business, learning from your mistakes, and celebrating your accomplishments.

Appendix A

The following organizations provide education and support to small businesses.

American Business Association
Hillsboro Executive North
350 Fairway Drive, Suite 200
Deerfield Beach, FL 33441
800/221-2168
www.aba-assn.com
membership@assnservices.com

American Business Women's
  Association
9100 Ward Parkway, Box 8728
Kansas City, MO 64114
816/361-6621
abwa@abwa.org
www.abwahq.org

American Management Association
48th Street and Broadway
New York, NY 10020
212/586-8100
www.amanet.org

Council of Better Business Bureaus
1515 Wilson Boulevard
Arlington, VA 22209
703/276-0100

Entrepreneurship Institute
3592 Corporate Drive, Suite 101
Columbus, OH 43231
614/895-1153
www.tei.net
tei@tei.net

Insurance Information Institute
110 Williams Street
New York, NY 10038
212/669-9200
www.iii.org

National Association for the Self-
  Employed (NASE)
2328 Gravel Road
Ft. Worth, TX 76118
800/232-6273
www.nase.org

National Business Association
P.O. Box 700728
Dallas, TX 75370
214/991-5381
www.nationalbusiness.org
info@nationalbusiness.org

National Federation of Independent
  Business (NFIB)
600 Maryland Ave. S.W., Suite 700
Washington, DC 20024
202/554-9000
www.nfib.com

National Small Business Association
1156 15th Street NW, Suite 1100
Washington, D.C. 20005
202/293-8830 or 800/345-6728
www.nsba.biz

Service Corps of Retired Executives
  (SCORE)
409 3rd Street SW 6th Floor
Washington, DC 20024
800/634-0245 or 703/487-3612
www.score.org

Small Business Assistance Center
554 Main Street
Worcester, MA 01608
508/756-3513

Small Business Development Centers
  (SBDCNET)
501 W. Durango Blvd.
San Antonio, TX 78207
210/458-2747 or 210/458-7840
sbdcnet.org

Small Business Legislative Council
1100 H Street NW, Suite 540
Washington, DC 20005
202/639-8500
www.sblc.org
email@sblc.org

Support Services Alliance
P.O. Box 130
Schoharie, NY 12157
518/295-7966
www.ssainfo.com
info@ssamembers.com

U.S. Chamber of Commerce
1615 H Street NW
Washington, DC 20062
800/638-6582or 202/659-6000
www.uschamber.com

U.S. Department of the Treasury
Internal Revenue Service
1500 Pennsylvania Avenue NW
Washington, DC 20220
800/829-3676or 202/622-2000
www.ustreas.gov

U.S. Small Business Administration
  (SBA)
409 E. 3rd Street SW
Washington, DC 20416
800-827-5722 or 202/205-6770
www.sba.gov

Appendix B

Medical Intake Form

    The following example of a medical intake form asks questions of clients for the purpose of composing a medical profile. This form, though thorough, is by no means exhaustive, and may not apply to your particular practice. Tailor you own form to suit your needs, and include everything you can think of that will be of benefit to you and your clients.

    In general you'll want to include the following:

PATIENT

Name

Address

City

State

Zip

Phone number/cell phone number

Email

Sex

Marital status:

    single, married, widow(er),

    divorced

Social security number

Date of birth

Occupation

Employer

Referred by

Primary care physician

Address

City

State

Zip

Phone

Person to contact in emergency

Relationship to patient

Address

Phone

INSURANCE CARRIER

Policy number:

Group ID number:

Address

City

State

Zip

Phone

Sample of Additional Information Needed

FOR PATIENTS IN GENERAL
Health issues (list all)
Medications (current)
Nutritional supplements/herbs
Ever hospitalized?
Frequent childhood illness/respiratory illnesses/breathing issues
Do you get sick often?
Coffee/smoking/drugs/alcohol
Dizziness/fainting/headaches/foggy head
Allergies/skin conditions/asthma
Hepatitis/gallbladder issues/hiv/venereal diseases
Blood pressure—high/how cholesterol/blood sugar
Varicose veins, circulation issues, heart palpitations, pain or tightness in the
    chest
Body pains/lymph nodes enlarged/ bloody discharge/easy bruising
Itching/ numbness/stiffness/spasm/shaking
Libido (sex drive)/energy level during day
Insomnia, excessive sleeping, heavy dreaming/nightmares
Urinary issues/bowel movement regular/irregular/constipation/diarrhea/loose
Appetite/cravings/thirst/sweating
Gas/bloated/acid regurgitation/nausea
Worry a lot, fearful, irritable/impatient, angry outbursts, sad
Dislike heat, cold, damp, dry
Anything else you want to mention?

FOR WOMEN
How old when started first menses (and stoppedif applies)?
Are you pregnant?
Are you on a birth control pill /which one/how long/any side effects?
Number of births/miscarriages/abortions/other surgeries?
Past pregnancy (list if any problems)?
Menstrual cycle (early, late, regular, none)?
Any vaginal discharges or spotting?
Ovulation time (pain or other symptoms)?
PMS (bloated, cramps, edema, moody)?
Length of bleeding (days)?
Amount of blood (heavy, scanty)?
Color of blood (pale, fresh, dark)?
Quality (watery, normal, sticky)?
Clots/cramps/feeling cold/hot flushing/low energy level?
Last OBGYN check up? Anything abnormal?
Breasts (swollen, fibrocystic, painful)?

Cysts/fibroids/endometriosis/abnormal pap smear?
Venereal diseases/vaginal discharge—white/yellow/other?
Family history of breast, uterine, etc. cancer?
Hormone blood results: estrogen, progesterone, thyroid, FSH/LH etc.?
Taking any hormones?
Checked for osteoporosis—results?
Menopausal symptoms—flushing, sweating, palpitations, dry vagina, insomnia,
    irritable, urinary issues?
History of smoking, blood clots, epilepsy, hypertension or heart attack?
History of sexual abuse (optional)?
History of depression?

PAIN MANAGEMENT
When did your pain start and where is it?
Is it injury/illness related/work injury? Explain.
How intense is the pain now? (on scale from 1-10, 1 being very little pain, 10
    being the most pain).Does it fluctuate during the day—describe?
What medical tests have you had for this condition(s)?
Have you had it treated (MD, chiropractor, etc.)?
History of your injuries/accidents/falls in your life span?
Are (were) you on any medication/herbs/supplements for this pain?
Is the pain static or does it travel?
Is it sharp, dull, achy?
Is it worse with movement/stillness, day/night, warm/cold, damp/dry/wind,
    emotional outburst—circle appropriate?
How much do you sit, stand, walk per day? Do you carry heavy objects?
Do you feel the pain is in the joints, muscles, bones, organs?
Do you do any sport activities?
Do you have a history of abnormal blood clotting or bleeding?
Do you have a history of heart condition, stroke, depression, chronic slow
    bowels, menstrual issues (clotting, cramps)?
Energy level/sleep quality?

MENOPAUSE
(Fill in and circle if applicable)
Hot flashes (use scale 1,2,3,4,5,6,7,8,9,10) and indicate when worse—morning,
afternoon, evening; worse when doing or feeling _____(fill in).
Fatigue/dry throat/mouth/no desire to drink
Depression/anxiety/irritability/nervousness/fright
Suffocating sensations/mood swings
Over-thinking/unable to think & concentrate/forgetfulness
Insomnia—cannot fall asleep, wake up often, restless sleep
Palpitations/hypertension/hot palms
Frequent urination/feeling of heaviness

Breast distention/cold nipples
Low back pain/hypochondriac pain/chest pain/hip pain
Dry vagina or discharge/painful intercourse/low libido
Heartburn/acid reflux
Headaches/light-headedness/dry eyes
Constipation/diarrhea/flatulence/bloating
Tongue and mouth sores
Menses—how often, amount, clots
Cold extremities/edema
Dizziness/vertigo

PREGNANCY
Name of your OB/GYN MD?
Person to contact in case of emergency?
List all your pregnancy related health issues?
List all the tests done to monitor your pregnancy?
Do you have insurance and which hospital (where) do you intend to give birth?
Can we contact your doctor for more information if needed?
    If yes, please, give contact information.
How long have you been pregnant?
How many children do you have (list their health issues if any)?
How many abortions?
How many miscarriages?
Were there any complications with previous pregnancies and/or the current
    pregnancy?
Where were you hospitalized for your pregnancy—currently or in the past?
Are you on any medication or herbal supplements?
Do you suffer from seizures?
Do you have high blood pressure, morning sickness, varicose veins, feel tired,
    hemorrhoids, low back pain, bowel problems, urinary issues?
Do you drink coffee/tea/alcohol or smoke?
Are you under lots of stress or suffer from anxiety, depression?
Do you get all the support you need/want?

FERTILITY FOR WOMEN
Do you have any children?
How long have you been trying to get pregnant?
Have you tried any method of assisted reproduction? If yes, list the MD and the
    procedure(s).
Any miscarriages/abortions/D&C/ectopic pregnancy/pelvic surgery (if yes,
    which part of pregnancy?)
Describe your history of birth control method.
Have you had any sexually transmitted diseases/viral infections/allergies/
    autoimmune diseases/cancer/candida overgrowth?

186

Hormone level test (FSH, LH, prolactin, estrogen, progesterone, thyroid)?

Any long term exposure to chemicals (and your husband?)

Are you stressed out? (on scale 1-10—1 being the least)?

Do you have anxiety/depression or other similar conditions?

Have you been diagnosed with fibroids, ovarian cysts, endometriosis, polycystic ovaries, pathological vaginal discharge, hypothyroidism, tilted uterus, etc.?

Ob/Gyn exams-any pathologies (last 10 years)?

Describe you menstrual cycle (regularity, length, amount)? Menarche (1st period):

Do you keep BBT or keep tract of your cycle?

Do you test yourself for ovulation (how)?

Sleep quality?

Do you get cold/hot easily?

Do you take medication/herbs/vitamins?

Has your partner been evaluated for sperm quality (list all the workup done)?

Do you have diabetes/high blood pressure or other health conditions?

FERTILITY FOR MEN

List current health issues

List chronic health issues

History of infections (plus list if you have had yeast, veneral diseases, HIV, Hepatitis,Mumps, etc.)

Do you have high blood pressure, diabetes, high cholesterol, or heart condition?

Have you had your sperm quality and quantity tested? Were you diagnosed with varicocele or sperm antibodies?

Have you had your hormones level checked (testosterone, LH, FSH, DHEA, cortisol)?

Do you drink alcohol, smoke, take recreational drugs (how often?)

Do you eat sugars or take stimulants-coffee, coke, tea-how much?

Have you taken any pharmaceutical drugs for a prolonged period of time? Have you used any steroids for muscle building?

Have you had any injury to your reproductive organs?

Have you worked with chemicals—consider both work and hobbies?

Do you suffer from depression or anxiety, and are very stressed out?

Do you have any of the following:

Inability to have an erection; loss of libido (sexual drive); inability to maintain an erection; prematureor none or difficult ejaculation; pain during intercourse

Are you in front of a computer/TV often? Do you do air travel often?

Mark if you have any of the following: lumbago, weak legs, low libido, copious clear urine, feel often tired, thirsty, bitter taste, cramps in the perineum, clouded urine, fullness in the epigastrium

Allergies (specify)

DETOX

Are you/were you in contact with toxic materials (work, pastime, hobby, etc.)
Do you live in a house that is over 25-years-old?
Have you had a recent remodeling done in your house? Did your health
   change?
Do you use dry cleaners often?
Do you commute long distances?
Do you sleep close to electronic equipment?
Do you play onpublic lawns frequently?
Do you have any neurological problems?
Do you get sick easily?
Check the following if you have them:
Skin rashes
Digestive problems
Fatigue and exhaustion
Swollen glands
Depression/anxiety
Irritability
Difficulty concentrating
Indecision
Numbness/tingling in extremities
Memory loss
Irregular heart beat
Headaches
Low-grade fever
Joint pains
Muscular disorders
Chest pain/pain under arms
Drowsiness
Dizziness
Candida/yeast infections
Diarrhea/constipation
Loss of appetite
Autoimmune disorders
Allergies
Weight loss/weight gain
Foul breath
Excessive sweating

*Many thanks to Dasha Trebichavska, L.Ac., who gave permission
to reprint her very thorough medical intake form.*

Appendix C

The credentials below refer to a variety of certifications degrees, registrations, programs, diplomas, and educational trainings. I've listed some of the most frequently used here, but this list is not exhaustive.

ABMP - Associated Bodywork and Massage Professionals

ACAT - American Center for the Alexander Technique

ACMT – Association of Certified Massage Therapists

ACST – Association of Certified Somatic Therapists

ADTR – Academy of Dance Therapists Registered

AOBTA – American Oriental Bodywork Therapy Association

AMSAT – American Society of Alexander Technique

AMTA – American Massage Therapy Association

ATR – Registered Art Therapist

ATR-BC – Board Certified Art Therapist

B.S.N. – Bachelor of Nursing

B.S.W. – Bachelor of Social Work

CADC – Certified Alcohol and Drug Counselor

CBPM – Certified Bonnie Pruden Myotherapist

CET – Certified Exercise Therapist

CIH – Certified Intuitive Healer

CMT – Certified Massage Therapist

CNMT – Certified Neuromuscular Therapist

CNS – Certified Nutritional Specialist

CRT – Certified Regression Therapist

CS – Clinical Specialist

CTPM – Certified Trigger Point Myotherapist

D.C. – Doctor of Chiropractic

D.O. – Doctor of Osteopathy

D.P.H. – Doctor of Public Health

GLBT – Gay, lesbian, bisexual, transgender

JSD – Certified Jin Shin Do Bodymind Acupressurist

LICSW – Licensed Social Worker

Lic.Ac. – Licensed Acupuncturist

LMHC – Licensed Mental Health Counselor

LMFT – Licensed Marriage and Family Therapist

LMT – Licensed Massage Therapist

M.A. – Master of Arts

M.C.A.T. – Master of Creative Arts Therapy

M.Div. – Master of Divinity

M.D. – Medical Doctor

M.Ed. – Master of Education

M.P.H. – Master of Public Health

M.S. – Master of Science

M.S.W. – Master of Social Work

M.S.N. – Master of Nursing

N.D. – Doctor of Naturopathy

NCACII – Nation Certified Alcoholism Counselor, Second Level

O.D. – Doctor of Optometry

OTRIL – Registered and Licensed Occupational Therapist

Ph.D. – Doctor of Philosophy

Psy.D. – Doctor of Psychology

PT – Physical Therapist

RD – Registered Dietician

RN – Registered Nurse

RPP – Registered Polarity Practitioner

RYT – Registered Yoga Therapist

Glossary of Holistic Practices

Acupressure - a form of therapy that employs the principles of acupuncture and Chinese medicine, using the same points on the body as acupuncture, but stimulating them with finger pressure instead of needles.

Acupuncture—the technique of inserting very small, sharp needles through the skin at certain points on the body, called pathways or meridians, to control pain and other symptoms associated with a disorder. Acupuncture is over 5,000 years old.

Alexander Technique—a method that educates patients on how to move during their daily activities without creating stiffness. Special emphasis is placed on learning balance and coordination in ways that foster ease of movement.

Alternative Medicine & Therapies—any medical treatments, practices, techniques, and products used to alleviate chronic conditions and ailments through the use of non-traditional medical applications.

Apitherapy—a therapy that applies bee stings to treat a wide variety of ailments. Bee venom supposedly stimulates the production of hormones in the body that have anti-inflammatory properties and is thought to be thousands of years old.

Applied Kinesiology—a modality that employs muscle-testing exercises to evaluate the body's physical state, developed by George J. Goodheart, Jr., a chiropractor, who believed that dysfunctional organs could be traced through muscle groups.

Aquatic Bodywork—the use of water in the form of pools, spas, hot tubs, and saunas for the purpose of treating chronic disorders, aiding recovery from surgery, easing muscle tension, rejuvenating the skin, and increasing flexibility.

Aromatherapy—a practice that uses essential or ethereal oils, and other aromatic compounds diluted from plants, to treat illnesses ranging from skin rashes to cancer. They are also frequently used as lubricants for massage, or burned as incense.

Art, Dance & Music Therapy—therapies designed to elicit repressed emotions and to resolve traumas through the use of painting, dance, and movement; as well as particular sounds or intonations. These therapies can be especially effective with children.

Asian Medicine & Therapies—refers primarily to Chinese, Japanese, and Ayurvedic medical applications and practices, often employing herbs, roots, teas, and other natural substances for healing.

Ayurvedic Medicine—Ayurveda, which means "the science of life," is a natural healing system using yoga and meditation as part of the healing practice. Developed in India, it addresses imbalances in the three doshas thought to make up the human form.

Biofeedback—a form of treatment that instructs patients on how to determine when and where their blood pressure and muscle tension are increasing through the use of a machine. Once identified by patients, these stressors can be controlled and/or eliminated.

Biological Dentistry—a practice identifying toxins, and hidden tooth and gum infections, as deleterious to overall health. In use for over 25 years in Germany, it has traced chronic degenerative illness to dental problems and traditional treatment techniques.

Bodywork Therapies—any therapy designed to manipulate, soothe, or realign the spine, muscles, and soft tissues in ways that foster ease of movement, flexibility, loss of pain and stiffness, increased tone and strength, and decreased illness and dysfunction.

Bowen Therapy—a holistic system of healing developed in Australia in the 1950s by Tom Bowen, that focuses on specific breathing techniques. Patients learn to relinquish traumatic memories, and achieve understanding of their own psychological makeup.

Breema—a form of physical therapy performed on the floor consisting of rhythmical movements and stretches. Designed to induce deep relaxation, and stimulation of the self-healing processes of the body, Breema adheres to nine Universal Principles.

Buteyko—a method of breathwork aimed at reducing the negative effects of asthma, bronchitis, emphysema, and allergies. Buteyko is used to treat wheezing, coughing, poor concentration, and the excessive production of mucus.

Chelation Therapy—a series of intravenous infusions aimed at reducing the effects of atherosclerosis and other serious health problems, such as lead poisoning, mercury poisoning, and other allegedly toxic conditions diagnosed by tests on blood and hair.

Chinese Medicine & Therapies—the use of Chinese herbs, roots, and plants prepared by ancient formulas handed down over the centuries for healing, as well as practices aimed at balancing the yin and yang (opposing forces) of the body.

Chiropractic Care—a health profession that treats, and attempts to prevent, mechanical malfunctions of the musculoskeletal system, and the effects these disorders have on the nervous system, through spinal adjustments and proper alignment of the vertebrae.

Colon Therapy—an procedure similar to an enema, using purified water sometimes infused with minerals, inserted into the colon for the purpose of removing the buildup of potentially harmful toxins.

Color Therapy (Chromotherapy)—the practice of applying of color and light to specific "acupoints' to promote healing. Because colors tend to elicit either positive or negative emotional reactions, they can be heightened or eliminated for therapeutic effect.

Craniosacral Therapy—a technique involving gentle manipulation of the bones of the skull, the underlying meningeal membranes, and the nerve endings in the scalp. It is used to treat a variety of conditions such as chronic pain, migraine headaches, and stroke.

Diet & Dietary Therapy—the use of herbs, supplements, fresh fruits, vegetables, and grains to bring about health. A particular diet may be prescribed by an alternative practitioner to eliminate allergies, or identify a food that is contributing to illness.

Energy Medicine—the practice of manipulating the field of energy thought to surround the human body, and affect the health of the individual. Energy medicine is used to improve overall health and a provide a deeper sense of well-being.

Environmental Medicine—the application of medical procedures aimed at treating and reducing illnesses resulting from environmental factors such as air and water pollution, allergens, carbon monoxide, radiation, and electromagnetic fields.

Enzyme Therapy—the use of food (plant) enzymes and pancreatic (animal) enzymes to improve digestion and the absorption of essential nutrients. Patients are instructed to follow diets packed with whole foods and grains along with enzyme supplements.

Equine Therapy—the use of horses to aid both physical and emotional disabilities. Developed in the 1950s, it's based on the notion that human interaction with horses, which are highly intuitive and provide unconditional love, facilitate healing.

Fasting Therapies—any therapy that recommends restraining from eating anything solid for a certain period of time. Fasting participants are carefully watched for electrolyte imbalances, and are often encouraged to drink juices or other healthy liquids.

Feldenkrais—bodywork using sequential movements as a means of developing flexibility, and improving posture. Feldenkrais is used to reduce pain, stiffness, and stress, and to increase self-awareness so as to eliminate habitual muscular patterns.

Feng Shui—the Chinese art of placement based on the opposing forces of yin and yang. The flow of life energy, or "chi' is thought to positively or negatively affect individual environments depending on where objects, like mirrors and furniture, are positioned.

Flower Essences—an approach developed by Dr. Edward Bach in the 1930s to balance emotional states by ingesting liquid extracts of various flowers and plants. Bach's flower remedies are used to create harmony, and eliminate conflicts at the spiritual level.

Folk Medicine—medical practices developed by lay people over the course of time, often handed down from one generation to the next. Developed by trial and error, many of these practices have been quite effect in treating illness and have a rich cultural tradition.

Gemstone Therapy—the use of gemstones, believed for centuries to have healing properties. Each therapeutic gem has a different healing purpose and users are encouraged to find the appropriate stone, touch it, and place it where it can be seen daily.

Geriatric Massage—also known as massotherapy, is a form of massage therapy that employs techniques specifically suited to the conditions frequently seen in older patients such as poor circulation, loss of mobility, diabetic neuropathy, pain—even memory loss.

Guided Imagery—a technique designed to engender healing through the use of mental visualization. Listening to a tape or an instructor, practitioners are encouraged to create scenarios that allow them to let go of the past, and cope with issues regarding their health.

Hakomi—Hawaiian massage, practiced for centuries by the Kahuna Masters of Huna Wisdom. This healing art reflects an ancient people who honored nature and each other, and who provided a valuable means of bringing paradise into daily living.

Hellerwork—a procedure named for Joseph Heller designed to return fluidity to the connective tissue, increase range of motion, and muscle relaxation. Hellerwork is effective in treating tennis elbow, carpal tunnel syndrome, bursitis and tendonitis.

Herbal Medicine—medicine that is derived from plants in powder, liquid, or diluted form to ease suffering from a wide range of ailments. Each plant has a different curative power, and may be combined with others to effect a recovery from illness.

Holistic Dentistry—the practice of assessing the health and well-being of the whole patient. Since 1978, the Holistic Dental Association has been providing support in the continuing education of practitioners who have a desire to expand their knowledge.

Holistic Medicine—the practice of medicine that encourages doctors to take the whole patient into account (body, mind, and spirit), and that encourages patients to believe in the body's natural ability to heal itself, and to take responsibility for their own well-being.

Homeopathy—a practice developed by Samuel Hahnemann in the 18th century, employing the notion that "like cures like." Using diluted substances that might actually cause disease, Hahnemann found that in very small doses, they alleviated it instead.

Huna or Ho'ala Huna—is the healing and spiritual system of ancient Hawaii, practiced for centuries by the Kahuna Masters, placing emphasis on discovering one's own nature and one's experience of the divine.

Hydrotherapy—the use of showers, baths, wraps, pools, spas, and saunas for the purpose of rehabilitation. Exercises performed in water, particularly with the additions of underwater jets and mineral salts, result in flexibility, and loss of pain and stiffness.

Hyperthermia Therapies—the practice of creating unusually high body temperature for treating different types of cancers and pre-cancerous conditions including those of the brain, esophagus, throat, lungs, breasts, stomach, intestines, and pancreas.

Hypnotherapy- the use of new instructions to the patient's subconscious mind, via relaxation techniques, in order to bring about changes in behavior, habits, phobias, and illnesses. Hypnotherapy also unlocks inner potential through metaphor and symbolism.

Infant Massage—refers to massage therapy specifically applied to full-term infants, infants born prematurely, and those with gastrointestinal problems, or motor impairment, by a trained and licensed massage therapist.

Iridology—the study of the iris of the eye for the purpose of determining the overall health of the body. It is thought that the patterns, markings, and colors found in the eye correspond to parts of the body and can indicate the presence of disease.

Juice Therapy—the ingestion of fruit and/or vegetable juices (and water) during a fast for the purpose of removing toxins from the body and restoring overall health. Some juice therapy also allows for a small amount of solids after a certain amount of time.

Light Therapy (Phototherapy)—is exposure to specific wavelengths of light using lasers, LEDs, fluorescent lamps, or very bright, full-spectrum light, for a prescribed amount of time to ease acne, seasonal affective disorder, and other maladies.

Lomi Lomi—one of the oldest forms of massage developed by ancient Polynesians, employing gentle, continuous strokes that reach deep into the muscle tissue, promoting relaxation, healing, and greater flexibility.

Macrobiotics—from "macro' meaning great, and "bio' meaning life, macrobiotics is the practice of achieving health and longevity through a diet that reflects a high respect for nature and the environment, and includes ways of selecting, preparing, and growing food.

Magnetic Field Therapy—also known as biomagnetic therapy, is a treatment for a wide variety of pain symptoms, that uses magnets or electromagnetic fields thought to enhance blood flow, and bring more oxygen to the affected region of the body.

Massage Therapy—the practice of manipulating, kneading, and soothing the muscles and soft tissues of the body for the purpose of loosening muscles, removing tension, increasing balance, and improving posture.

Meditation—the practice of stilling the mind for a period of time by sitting in contemplation, often using a mantra or prayer to begin. Meditation is a very effective tool for reducing stress, lowering blood pressure, and attuning to the spiritual realm.

Myotherapy—a method that applies pressure at hypersensitive locations in the muscles that cause pain (trigger points). Trigger points may be caused by injuries, disease, or physical or emotional stress.

Naprapathy—a drug-free method of treatment that involves the manipulation of muscles, tendons, and ligaments for the alleviation and prevention of problems that originate in the connective tissues.

Naturopathic Medicine—a medical practice that uses the body's own ability to heal. Naturopathic physicians employ natural remedies, herbal medicine, homeopathy, etc., and emphasize the importance of diet and lifestyle in achieving total health.

Neural Therapy—a system of treatment aimed at relieving pain caused by the misfiring of the body's electrical circuitry. Anesthetics are injected to increase the flow of energy, normalize the function of cells, and neutralize sensations of pain.

Neuro-Linguistic Programming—a treatment that provides verbal instructions to a patient attempting to modify certain behaviors, and to develop communication and persuasion skills. NLP also uses images, sounds, and hypnosis for workplace motivation.

Neuromuscular Therapy (NMT)—a form of manual therapy concerned with the nervous system and its effect on the muscular and skeletal systems, that uses pressure on specific myofascial points, kinesiology, and biomechanics to relieve pain.

Nutritional Supplements—the wide assortment of minerals, vitamins, wildflowers, plants, amino acids, fatty acids, and medicinal herbs that are taken in addition to a regular diet in pill, liquid or powder form for the purpose of increasing health and vitality.

Ortho-Bionomy—a method of gentle manipulation that enables clients to experience for themselves the body's tendency to tighten, so as to learn ways to correct structural and postural imbalances, heal chronic stress, and alleviate pain resulting from injury.

Orthomolecular Medicine—the practice of providing optimal amounts of natural substances to the body that act in accordance with the biochemical pathways to eradicate diseases such as atherosclerosis, schizophrenia, hypertension, cancer, and depression.

Osteopathic Medicine—a system of healthcare based on the idea that anatomical abnormalities are associated with physiological problems. Osteopathy relies on manipulative techniques to correct body structures that might cause disease.

Oxygen Therapy—the practice of breathing any gas, for medical purposes, which contains at least 21% oxygen. Administered from a tank, oxygen alters the body chemistry to promote repair, and can be effective for cluster headaches and arthritis.

Physiotherapy—the practice of supervised exercise that takes place in a pool of warm water, usually at a temperature of between 92 and 99 degrees Fahrenheit, for the purpose of building and rebuilding muscular strength.

Polarity Therapy—a hands-on approach to balancing the human energy field, facilitating the release of energy blocks and deep-seated tensions. Techniques include circular pressure on sensitive contact points, light rhythmic rocking, and stretching motions.

Pranic Healing—uses ki, chi, or prana, the life force energy, to flow through areas known variously as acupoints, chakras, meridians, pathways or "bioplasmic channels' to eliminate blockages in the energy field, and to promote the unimpeded movement of prana.

Qigong—an ancient Chinese healing art using a series of focused exercises to increase stamina, flexibility, and relaxation. Qigong combines movement, meditation, and the regulation of breathing to enhance the flow of energy.

Reflexology—an ancient Chinese technique that uses pressure-point massage primarily on the feet, but also on the hands and ears, to restore the flow of energy. It's believed that pressure points on the feet, hands, and ears correspond to organs in the body.

Reiki—a system of hands-on healing developed in the early 1900's by Mikao Usui in Japan, now passed from Master to student. Reiki is said to bring energy into the body for deep relaxation and healing by channeling spiritual energy through the practitioner.

Rolfing—a method of therapeutic manipulation aimed at realigning the connective tissue that binds organs and muscles together, developed by Ida P. Rolf. Rolfing is based on the assumption that structure profoundly affects physiological processes.

Rosen Method—developed by Marion Rosen, a physical therapist, the Rosen Method uses gentle touch and verbal communication to help patients release suppressed emotions, which frees up corresponding muscular tension throughout the body.

Rubenfeld—a body-integrated therapy that uses the power of touch to release the deep emotions, connections and self-awareness necessary for true healing. Rubenfeld includes talk, imagery, hypnosis, movement, and the interpretation of dreams.

Sclerology—the science and art of reading the markings in the whites of the eyes as indicators of illness and disease, used by indigenous cultures for centuries. According to adherents, sclerology can reveal conditions within days of their occurrence.

Shen Therapy—an effective therapy using naturally occurring chi from a practitioner's hands to relax and release both physical and emotional pain held in the body. It promotes relaxation, reduces stress, and is useful for the development of personal growth.

Shiatsu—a traditional Japanese hands-on massage employing pressure-point massage techniques to stimulate meridians thought to carry life energy. Practitioners apply rhythmic finger pressure at specific points to treat pain and illness.

Somatic Education—literally the re-education of muscles and soft tissue that have over time become cramped, shortened, or otherwise impaired due to overuse, injury, or constant tension. Somatic education is often used to treat fibromyalgia.

Sound Therapy—an approach to healing by creating change at the molecular vibratory level by employing low frequency sound and vibration. It offers a simple way get information about the body in order to assess the biochemical effects of stress.

Stress Management—any of a number of approaches to calming the "fight or flight" reaction of the body to events we deem outside our control. These include deep breathing, meditation, the use of biofeedback, yoga, massage, and flotations tanks.

Structural Integration—a means of working with the internal core of the body through a series of manipulations aimed at freeing up areas of chronic muscle tightness and congestion, creating greater freedom of movement.

T'ai Chi—a ancient traditional Chinese relaxation system consisting of 108 intricate exercises performed in a graceful manner over a 30-minute period, to improve and maintain health, and to enhance immune functions.

Thai Massage—a form of massage that originated in India over 2,500 years ago, then became popular in Thailand. It's based on "sen' or energy lines, which send energy thorough the body by the compression and manipulation of certain points.

Therapeutic Touch (TT)—invented by Dolores Krieger in the early 1970s, TT employs the energy of the practitioner to affect the energy field surrounding the patient for the purpose of stimulating a patient's own healing response.

Tibetan Medicine—a healing system similar to Ayurveda and Chinese medicine, it includes acupuncture and moxibustion, to heal both the physical and psychic being. It draws on the three principles of wind, bile, and phlegm, and also includes reincarnation.

Trepanation—also known as trephinning or trepanning, is a form of surgery during which a hole is drilled or scraped into the skull in order to treat problems related to intercranial diseases, or give practitioners access for certain neurological procedures.

Tui Na—a form of Chinese acupressure that uses many hand strokes applied to acupressure points, channels and muscle groups, to transfer the healthy chi of the practitioner to the ailing patient.

Yoga—the Hindu system of exercise, breathing, and contemplation for achieving union or "yoga" with the supreme spiritual consciousness. The regular practice of yoga reduces blood pressure, increases strength and balance, and creates a sense of mental calm.

Bibliography

Alarid, William M.; *Money Sources for Small Business: How You Can Find Private, State, Federal, and Corporate Financing*; Puma Publishing; Santa Maria, CA; 1991.

Albion, Mark S.; *True to Yourself: Leading a Values-Based Business*; Berrett-Koehler; San Francisco, CA; 2006.

Alternative Link; *The State Legal Guide to Complementary and Alternative Medicine*; Cengage Delmar Learning; Clifton Park, NY; 2001

Berkeley Holistic Health Center; *The Holistic Health Life Book: A Guide to Personal and Planetary Well-Being*, And/Or Press; Berkeley, CA; 1981.

Chopra, Deepak; *Perfect Health*; Random House; New York, NY; 1991.

Chopra, Deepak; *The Seven Spiritual Laws of Success: A Practical Guide to the Fulfillment of Your Dreams*; Amber-Allen Publishing; San Raphael, CA; 1994.

Cohen, Michael H.; *Legal Issues in Alternative Medicine: A Guide for Clinicians, Hospitals, and Patients*; Trafford Publishing; Victoria, British Columbia, Canada; 2003.

Craven, Jackie; *The Healthy Home*; Rockport Publishers; Gloucester, MA; 2003.

DeLuca, Fred; *Start Small, Finish Big: Fifteen Key Lessons to Start—And Run—Your Own Successful Business*; Warner Books; New York, NY; 2000.

Dwyer, Christopher; *The Small Business Administration*; Chealsea House Publishers; New York, NY; 1990.

Froemming, Paul; *The Best Guide to Alternative Medicine*; Renaissance Books; Los Angeles, CA; 1998.

Future Medicine, Inc.; *Alternative Medicine*; Future Medicine, Inc.; Puyallup, WA; 1993.

Gordon, Kim T.; *Maximum Marketing, Minimum Dollars: The Top 50 Ways to Grow Your Small Business*; Kaplan Publishing; Chicago, IL; 2006.

Jasper, Margaret C.; *Law For the Small Business Owner*; Oceana Publications; Dobbs Ferry, NY; 1994.

Levinson, Jay Conrad; *Guerilla Marketing Excellence: The 50 Golden Rules for Small Business Success*; Houghton Mifflin Co.; Boston, MA; 1993.

Morris, Tom; *If Aristotle Ran General Motors*; Henry Holt and Company; New York, NY; 1997.

Pinson, Linda; *Keeping the Books: Basic Recordkeeping and Accounting for the Successful Small Business*; Dearborn Trade; Chicago, IL; 2001.

Sered, Susan Starr; *Uninsured in America: Life and Death in the Land of Opportunity*; University of California Press; Berkeley, CA; 2005.

Siegel, Gonnie McClung; *How to Advertise and Promote Your Small Business;* Wiley and Sons; New York, NY; 1978.

Sohnen-Moe, Cherie; *Business Mastery*; Cheri Sohnen-Moe Associates, Tucson, AZ; 1989.

Stone, Julie; *An Ethical Framework for Complementary and Alternative Therapists*; Routledge, New York, NY; 2002.

Sullivan, Robert; *The Small Business Start-Up Guide*; Information International; Great Falls, VA; 2000.

Swerdlow, Joel L.; *Nature's Medicine: Plants that Heal*; National Geographic Society, Washington, D.C.; 2000.

Trivieri, Larry; *The American Holistic Medical Association Guide to Holistic Healing Therapies for Optimal Wellness*; Wiley and Sons, New York, NY; 2001.

Weil, Andrew; *Eight Weeks to Optimum Health*; AlfredA. Knopf Publishing; New York, NY; 1997.

Websites

Borgerd, Gail, MedicClaim Consultants, LLC *Understanding and Dealing with Health Insurance Companies and Health Care Providers*; July 24, 2007

www.aapb.org/i4a/pages/index.cfm?pageid=1; July 5, 2007

www.acupuncture.com/statelaws/statelaw.htm; June 12, 2007

www.acupuncturetoday.com/archives2000/feb/02homeopathy.html; June 17, 2007

www.acupuncturetoday.com/schools; June 7, 2007

www.alternativemedicine.com/retailer/store_templates/shell_id_1.asp?storeID; June 28, 2007

www.amerchiro.org; July 10, 2007

www.answers.com/topic/acupressure; June 7, 2007

www.artistsfoundation.org/art_pages/resources/resources_healthcare_generalhc.ht; July 18, 2007

www.bodytherapyassociates.com/order.php; July 11, 2007

www.bostonabcd.org/houseman/houseman.pdf; June 17, 2007

www.business.gov; June 6, 2007

www.crawfordbroadcasting.com/~kkpz/whyradio.htm; June 7, 2007

www.ecomall.com; June 27, 2007

www.edu411.org/programs/Alternative_&_Holistic/
?kw=A_Healthcare_Holistic&gclid=CNjci_axto0CFQJ_HgodlzRJHQ;
July 14, 2007

www.entrepreneur.com/startingabusiness/businessplans/article38308.html; June 26, 2007

www.globalintegrativehealth.org/holisticpsychotherapy.php; July 11, 2007

www.gm.com; June 15, 2007

www.greenpeople.org: June 24, 2007

www.happyhippie.com; June 15, 2007

www.heavenfelts.com/spiritcolour.html; June 16, 2007

www.hemingwaymassageproducts.com; June 16, 2007

www.homeopathic.com/articles/intro/history.php; July 5, 2007

www.homeopathic.org/resource_prof.htm: June 15, 2007

www.hpso.com; July 17, 2007

www.hrsbdc.org.vectec.org/marketing/media/directmail; July 14, 2007

www.hud.gov/local/shared/news/smbusiness.cfm?state=ri; June 7, 2007

www.iahp.com; July 2, 2007

www.iama.edu/Articles/Acupuncture_Statistics.htm; June 19, 2007

www.injuryboard.com/view.cfm/Topic=32; July 11, 2007

www.itmonline.org/arts/restructure.htm; June 19,2007

www.looksmartalternative.com; June 15, 2007

www.massageking.com/categories; July 12, 2007

www.massagenaturals.com; June 22, 2007

www.massageresource.com/ubbcgi; July 13, 2007

www.massagetherapy.com/media/metricsgrowth.php; June 15, 2007

www.mb.thehartford.com/reduce_risk/risk_tips_professional.asp; July 11, 2007

www.nase.org; June 25, 2007

www.naturalhealers.com/?google=massage_therapy_schools_phr; June 17, 2007

www.naturesbridge.com/holisticmed.html: July 18, 2007

www.ncbtmb.com; July 10, 2007

www.ncbtmb.com/press_releases/60k_certificants.html; June 23, 2007

www.nccam.nih.gov: June 24, 2007

www.nfib.com/object/io_16774.html; July 17, 2007

www.nih.gov; June 11, 2007

www.njconsumeraffairs.gov/nursing/mass.htm; July 14, 2007

www.processes.org/holistic.php; June 11, 2007

www.psychologytoday.com/articles/pto-20040302-000003.html; June 13, 2007

www.rab.com/station/mediafact/mfyellow.html; June 9, 2007

www.smallbusinessresources.com; July 5, 2007

www.thegreenguide.com; June 28, 1007

www.theorganicreport.com/pages/418_organic_linens.cfm; July 12, 2007

www.touchoffreedom.com/bodywork.html; June 25, 2007

www.trager.com; June 12, 2007

www.usatoday.com/money/media/2005-07-12-digital-tv-usat_x.htm; June 9, 2007

www.wholehealtheducation.com/news/newsarchive/may2005.shtml; June 16, 2007

www.wholehealthnow.com/homeopathy_pro/homeopathy_1975.html;
   June 14, 2007

www.workmanscompinsurance.net; June 17, 2007

www.xdrive.com; July 28, 2007

Index

Notes

Notes

LaVergne, TN USA
03 December 2010
207203LV00004B/92/P